Gradle Dependency Management

Learn how to use Gradle's powerful dependency management through extensive code samples, and discover how to define, customize, and deploy dependencies

Hubert Klein Ikkink

community experience distilled

BIRMINGHAM - MUMBAI

Gradle Dependency Management

First published: June 2015

Production reference: 1120615

Published by Packt Publishing Ltd.
Livery Place
35 Livery Street
Birmingham B3 2PB, UK.

ISBN 978-1-78439-278-9

www.packtpub.com

Credits

Author
Hubert Klein Ikkink

Reviewers
Tony Dieppa
Izzet Mustafaiev
Konstantin Zgirovskiy

Commissioning Editor
Pramila Balan

Acquisition Editor
Sonali Vernekar

Content Development Editor
Athira Laji

Technical Editor
Siddhesh Ghadi

Copy Editor
Sarang Chari

Project Coordinator
Harshal Ved

Proofreader
Safis Editing

Indexer
Monica Mehta

Production Coordinator
Arvindkumar Gupta

Cover Work
Arvindkumar Gupta

About the Author

Hubert Klein Ikkink, born in 1973, lives in Tilburg, the Netherlands, with his beautiful wife and three gorgeous children. He is also known as mrhaki, which is simply the initials of his name prepended by "mr". He studied information systems and management at Tilburg University. After finishing his studies in 1996, he started to develop Java software. Over the years, his focus switched from applets to servlets, and from Java Enterprise Edition applications to Spring-based software and Groovy-related technologies. He likes the expressiveness of the Groovy language and how it is used in other tools, such as Gradle. He also wrote *Gradle Effective Implementation Guide, Packt Publishing*.

In the Netherlands, Hubert works for a company called JDriven. JDriven focuses on technologies that simplify and improve the development of enterprise applications. Employees of JDriven have years of experience with Java and related technologies and are all eager to learn about new technologies. Hubert works on projects using Grails and Java combined with Groovy and Gradle.

About the Reviewers

Izzet Mustafaiev is a family guy who likes to throw BBQ parties and travel.

Professionally, he is a software engineer working at EPAM Systems with primary skills in Java and hands-on experience in Groovy/Ruby, and is exploring FP with Erlang/Elixir. Izzet has participated in different projects as a developer and as an architect. He advocates XP, clean code, and DevOps practices when he speaks at engineering conferences.

Konstantin Zgirovskiy grew up alongside Android, in a manner of speaking. In 2008, he started programming web services and Chrome extensions for an online browser game, which was later made official. In 2011, Konstantin continued to explore Android through writing a game, which brought him victory in a local programming contest. Nowadays, he works at Looksery, Inc., where he is involved in developing an app with face-tracking and transformation technology for video chats, video selfies, and images on mobile devices.

I would like to thank my cats, friends, colleagues, and family for their support. My thanks also go to Packt Publishing for this opportunity. Additionally, I would like to thank Dasha Tsareva-Lenskaya for motivating and encouraging me whenever I got distracted.

www.PacktPub.com

Support files, eBooks, discount offers, and more

For support files and downloads related to your book, please visit www.PacktPub.com.

Did you know that Packt offers eBook versions of every book published, with PDF and ePub files available? You can upgrade to the eBook version at www.PacktPub.com, and as a print book customer, you are entitled to a discount on the eBook copy. Get in touch with us at service@packtpub.com for more details.

At www.PacktPub.com, you can also read a collection of free technical articles, sign up for a range of free newsletters, and receive exclusive discounts and offers on Packt books and eBooks.

https://www2.packtpub.com/books/subscription/packtlib

Do you need instant solutions to your IT questions? PacktLib is Packt's online digital book library. Here, you can search, access, and read Packt's entire library of books.

Why subscribe?

- Fully searchable across every book published by Packt
- Copy and paste, print, and bookmark content
- On demand and accessible via a web browser

Free access for Packt account holders

If you have an account with Packt at www.PacktPub.com, you can use this to access PacktLib today and view 9 entirely free books. Simply use your login credentials for immediate access.

Table of Contents

Preface

When we write code in our Java or Groovy project, we mostly have dependencies on other projects or libraries. For example, we could use the Spring framework in our project, so we are dependent on classes found in the Spring framework. We want to be able to manage such dependencies from Gradle, our build automation tool.

We will see how we can define and customize the dependencies we need. We learn not only how to define the dependencies, but also how to work with repositories that store the dependencies. Next, we will see how to customize the way Gradle resolves dependencies.

Besides being dependent on other libraries, our project can also be a dependency for other projects. This means that we need to know how to deploy our project artifacts so that other developers can use it. We learn how to define artifacts and how to deploy them to, for example, a Maven or Ivy repository.

What this book covers

Chapter 1, Defining Dependencies, introduces dependency configurations as a way to organize dependencies. You will learn about the different types of dependencies in Gradle.

Chapter 2, Working with Repositories, covers how we can define repositories that store our dependencies. We will see not only how to set the location, but also the layout of a repository.

Chapter 3, Resolving Dependencies, is about how Gradle resolves our dependencies. You will learn how to customize the dependency resolution and resolve conflicts between dependencies.

Chapter 4, Publishing Artifacts, covers how to define artifacts for our project to be published as dependencies for others. We will see how to use configurations to define artifacts. We also use a local directory as a repository to publish the artifacts.

Chapter 5, Publishing to a Maven Repository, looks at how to publish our artifacts to a Maven repository. You will learn how to define a publication for a Maven-like repository, such as Artifactory or Nexus, and how to use the new and incubating publishing feature of Gradle.

Chapter 6, Publishing to Bintray, covers how to deploy our artifacts to Bintray. Bintray calls itself a Distribution as a Service and provides a low-level way to publish our artifacts to the world. In this chapter, we will look at how to use the Bintray Gradle plugin to publish our artifacts.

Chapter 7, Publishing to an Ivy Repository, is about publishing our artifacts to an Ivy repository. We will look into the different options to publish our artifacts to an Ivy repository, which is actually quite similar to publishing to a Maven repository.

What you need for this book

In order to work with Gradle and the code samples in this book, we need at least Java Development Kit (version 1.6 or higher), Gradle (samples are written with Gradle 2.3), and a good text editor.

Who this book is for

This book is for you if you are working on Java or Groovy projects and are using, or are going to use, Gradle to build your code. If your code depends on other projects or libraries, you will learn how to define and customize those dependencies. Your code can also be used by other projects, so you want to publish your project as a dependency for others whom you want to read this book.

Conventions

In this book, you will find a number of text styles that distinguish between different kinds of information. Here are some examples of these styles and an explanation of their meaning.

Code words in text, database table names, folder names, filenames, file extensions, pathnames, dummy URLs, user input, and Twitter handles are shown as follows: "We can include other contexts through the use of the `include` directive."

A block of code is set as follows:

```
// Define new configurations for build.
configurations {

    // Define configuration vehicles.
    vehicles {
        description = 'Contains vehicle dependencies'
    }

    traffic {
        extendsFrom vehicles
        description = 'Contains traffic dependencies'
    }

}
```

Any command-line input or output is written as follows:

```
$ gradle bintrayUpload
:generatePomFileForSamplePublication
:compileJava
:processResources UP-TO-DATE
:classes
:jar
:publishSamplePublicationToMavenLocal
:bintrayUpload

BUILD SUCCESSFUL

Total time: 9.125 secs
```

New terms and **important words** are shown in bold. Words that you see on the screen, for example, in menus or dialog boxes, appear in the text like this: "From this screen, we click on the **New package** button."

Reader feedback

Feedback from our readers is always welcome. Let us know what you think about this book—what you liked or disliked. Reader feedback is important for us as it helps us develop titles that you will really get the most out of.

To send us general feedback, simply e-mail feedback@packtpub.com, and mention the book's title in the subject of your message.

If there is a topic that you have expertise in and you are interested in either writing or contributing to a book, see our author guide at www.packtpub.com/authors.

Customer support

Now that you are the proud owner of a Packt book, we have a number of things to help you to get the most from your purchase.

Downloading the example code

You can download the example code files from your account at http://www.packtpub.com for all the Packt Publishing books you have purchased. If you purchased this book elsewhere, you can visit http://www.packtpub.com/support and register to have the files e-mailed directly to you.

Downloading the color images of this book

We also provide you with a PDF file that has color images of the screenshots/diagrams used in this book. The color images will help you better understand the changes in the output. You can download this file from https://www.packtpub.com/sites/default/files/downloads/B03462_Coloredimages.pdf.

Errata

Although we have taken every care to ensure the accuracy of our content, mistakes do happen. If you find a mistake in one of our books—maybe a mistake in the text or the code—we would be grateful if you could report this to us. By doing so, you can save other readers from frustration and help us improve subsequent versions of this book. If you find any errata, please report them by visiting http://www.packtpub.com/submit-errata, selecting your book, clicking on the **Errata Submission Form** link, and entering the details of your errata. Once your errata are verified, your submission will be accepted and the errata will be uploaded to our website or added to any list of existing errata under the Errata section of that title.

To view the previously submitted errata, go to https://www.packtpub.com/books/content/support and enter the name of the book in the search field. The required information will appear under the **Errata** section.

Piracy

Piracy of copyrighted material on the Internet is an ongoing problem across all media. At Packt, we take the protection of our copyright and licenses very seriously. If you come across any illegal copies of our works in any form on the Internet, please provide us with the location address or website name immediately so that we can pursue a remedy.

Please contact us at copyright@packtpub.com with a link to the suspected pirated material.

We appreciate your help in protecting our authors and our ability to bring you valuable content.

Questions

If you have a problem with any aspect of this book, you can contact us at questions@packtpub.com, and we will do our best to address the problem.

1
Defining Dependencies

When we develop software, we need to write code. Our code consists of packages with classes, and those can be dependent on the other classes and packages in our project. This is fine for one project, but we sometimes depend on classes in other projects we didn't develop ourselves, for example, we might want to use classes from an Apache Commons library or we might be working on a project that is part of a bigger, multi-project application and we are dependent on classes in these other projects.

Most of the time, when we write software, we want to use classes outside of our project. Actually, we have a dependency on those classes. Those dependent classes are mostly stored in archive files, such as **Java Archive (JAR)** files. Such archive files are identified by a unique version number, so we can have a dependency on the library with a specific version.

In this chapter, you are going to learn how to define dependencies in your Gradle project. We will see how we can define the configurations of dependencies. You will learn about the different dependency types in Gradle and how to use them when you configure your build.

Declaring dependency configurations

In Gradle, we define dependency configurations to group dependencies together. A dependency configuration has a name and several properties, such as a description and is actually a special type of `FileCollection`. Configurations can extend from each other, so we can build a hierarchy of configurations in our build files. Gradle plugins can also add new configurations to our project, for example, the Java plugin adds several new configurations, such as `compile` and `testRuntime`, to our project. The `compile` configuration is then used to define the dependencies that are needed to compile our source tree. The dependency configurations are defined with a `configurations` configuration block. Inside the block, we can define new configurations for our build. All configurations are added to the project's `ConfigurationContainer` object.

In the following example build file, we define two new configurations, where the traffic configuration extends from the vehicles configuration. This means that any dependency added to the vehicles configuration is also available in the traffic configuration. We can also assign a description property to our configuration to provide some more information about the configuration for documentation purposes. The following code shows this:

```
// Define new configurations for build.
configurations {

  // Define configuration vehicles.
  vehicles {
    description = 'Contains vehicle dependencies'
  }

  traffic {
    extendsFrom vehicles
    description = 'Contains traffic dependencies'
  }

}
```

To see which configurations are available in a project, we can execute the dependencies task. This task is available for each Gradle project. The task outputs all the configurations and dependencies of a project. Let's run this task for our current project and check the output:

```
$ gradle -q dependencies


------------------------------------------------------------
Root project
------------------------------------------------------------


traffic - Contains traffic dependencies
No dependencies

vehicles - Contains vehicle dependencies
No dependencies
```

Note that we can see our two configurations, traffic and vehicles, in the output. We have not defined any dependencies to these configurations, as shown in the output.

The Java plugin adds a couple of configurations to a project, which are used by the tasks from the Java plugin. Let's add the Java plugin to our Gradle build file:

```
apply plugin: 'java'
```

To see which configurations are added, we invoke the dependencies task and look at the output:

```
$ gradle -q dependencies


------------------------------------------------------------
Root project
------------------------------------------------------------


archives - Configuration for archive artifacts.
No dependencies

compile - Compile classpath for source set 'main'.
No dependencies

default - Configuration for default artifacts.
No dependencies

runtime - Runtime classpath for source set 'main'.
No dependencies

testCompile - Compile classpath for source set 'test'.
No dependencies

testRuntime - Runtime classpath for source set 'test'.
No dependencies
```

We see six configurations in our project just by adding the Java plugin. The archives configuration is used to group the artifacts our project creates. The other configurations are used to group the dependencies for our project. In the following table, the dependency configurations are summarized:

Name	Extends	Description
compile	none	These are dependencies to compile.
runtime	compile	These are runtime dependencies.
testCompile	compile	These are extra dependencies to compile tests.

Name	Extends	Description
testRuntime	runtime, testCompile	These are extra dependencies to run tests.
default	runtime	These are dependencies used by this project and artifacts created by this project.

Later in the chapter, we will see how we can work with the dependencies assigned to the configurations. In the next section, we will learn how to declare our project's dependencies.

Declaring dependencies

We defined configurations or applied a plugin that added new configurations to our project. However, a configuration is empty unless we add dependencies to the configuration. To declare dependencies in our Gradle build file, we must add the `dependencies` configuration block. The configuration block will contain the definition of our dependencies. In the following example Gradle build file, we define the `dependencies` block:

```
// Dependencies configuration block.
dependencies {
    // Here we define our dependencies.
}
```

Inside the configuration block, we use the name of a dependency configuration followed by the description of our dependencies. The name of the dependency configuration can be defined explicitly in the build file or can be added by a plugin we use. In Gradle, we can define several types of dependencies. In the following table, we will see the different types we can use:

Dependency type	Description
External module dependency	This is a dependency on an external module or library that is probably stored in a repository.
Client module dependency	This is a dependency on an external module where the artifacts are stored in a repository, but the meta information about the module is in the build file. We can override meta information using this type of dependency.
Project dependency	This is a dependency on another Gradle project in the same build.
File dependency	This is a dependency on a collection of files on the local computer.

Dependency type	Description
Gradle API dependency	This is a dependency on the Gradle API of the current Gradle version. We use this dependency when we develop Gradle plugins and tasks.
Local Groovy dependency	This is a dependency on the Groovy libraries used by the current Gradle version. We use this dependency when we develop Gradle plugins and tasks.

External module dependencies

External module dependencies are the most common dependencies in projects. These dependencies refer to a module in an external repository. Later in the book, we will find out more about repositories, but basically, a repository stores modules in a central location. A module contains one or more artifacts and meta information, such as references to the other modules it depends on.

We can use two notations to define an external module dependency in Gradle. We can use a string notation or a map notation. With the map notation, we can use all the properties available for a dependency. The string notation allows us to set a subset of the properties but with a very concise syntax.

In the following example Gradle build file, we define several dependencies using the string notation:

```
// Define dependencies.
dependencies {
  // Defining two dependencies.
  vehicles 'com.vehicles:car:1.0', 'com.vehicles:truck:2.0'

  // Single dependency.
  traffic 'com.traffic:pedestrian:1.0'
}
```

The string notation has the following format: **moduleGroup:moduleName:version**. Before the first colon, the module group name is used, followed by the module name, and the version is mentioned last.

If we use the map notation, we use the names of the attributes explicitly and set the value for each attribute. Let's rewrite our previous example build file and use the map notation:

```
// Compact definition of configurations.
configurations {
  vehicles
  traffic.extendsFrom vehicles
```

```
}

// Define dependencies.
dependencies {
  // Defining two dependencies.
  vehicles(
    [group: 'com.vehicles', name: 'car', version: '1.0'],
    [group: 'com.vehicles', name: 'truck', version: '2.0'],
  )

  // Single dependency.
  traffic group: 'com.traffic', name: 'pedestrian', version:
  '1.0'
}
```

We can specify extra configuration attributes with the map notation, or we can add an extra configuration closure. One of the attributes of an external module dependency is the `transitive` attribute. We learn more about how to work with transitive dependencies in *Chapter 3, Resolving Dependencies*. In the next example build file, we will set this attribute using the map notation and a configuration closure:

```
dependencies {
  // Use transitive attribute in map notation.
  vehicles group: 'com.vehicles', name: 'car',
      version: '1.0', transitive: false

  // Combine map notation with configuration closure.
  vehicles(group: 'com.vehicles', name: 'car', version: '1.0') {
    transitive = true
  }

  // Combine string notation with configuration closure.
  traffic('com.traffic:pedestrian:1.0') {
    transitive = false
  }
}
```

In the rest of this section, you will learn about more attributes you can use to configure a dependency.

Once of the advantages of Gradle is that we can write Groovy code in our build file. This means that we can define methods and variables and use them in other parts of our Gradle file. This way, we can even apply refactoring to our build file and make maintainable build scripts. Note that in our examples, we included multiple dependencies with the `com.vehicles` group name. The value is defined twice, but we can also create a new variable with the group name and reference of the variable in the dependencies configuration. We define a variable in our build file inside an `ext` configuration block. We use the `ext` block in Gradle to add extra properties to an object, such as our project.

The following sample code defines an extra variable to hold the group name:

```
// Define project property with
// dependency group name 'com.vehicles'
ext {
  groupNameVehicles = 'com.vehicles'
}

dependencies {
  // Using Groovy string support with
  // variable substition.
  vehicles "$groupNameVehicles:car:1.0"

  // Using map notation and reference
  // property groupNameVehicles.
  vehicles group: groupNameVehicles, name: 'truck', version:
  '2.0'
}
```

If we define an external module dependency, then Gradle tries to find a module descriptor in a repository. If the module descriptor is available, it is parsed to see which artifacts need to be downloaded. Also, if the module descriptor contains information about the dependencies needed by the module, those dependencies are downloaded as well. Sometimes, a dependency has no descriptor in the repository, and it is only then that Gradle downloads the artifact for that dependency.

A dependency based on a Maven module only contains one artifact, so it is easy for Gradle to know which artifact to download. But for a Gradle or Ivy module, it is not so obvious, because a module can contain multiple artifacts. The module will have multiple configurations, each with different artifacts. Gradle will use the configuration with the name `default` for such modules. So, any artifacts and dependencies associated with the `default` configuration are downloaded. However, it is possible that the `default` configuration doesn't contain the artifacts we need. We, therefore, can specify the `configuration` attribute for the dependency configuration to specify a specific configuration that we need.

The following example defines a `configuration` attribute for the dependency configuration:

```
dependencies {
  // Use the 'jar' configuration defined in the
  // module descriptor for this dependency.
  traffic group: 'com.traffic',
      name: 'pedestrian',
```

```
        version: '1.0',
        configuration: 'jar'


    }
```

When there is no module descriptor for a dependency, only the artifact is
downloaded by Gradle. We can use an artifact-only notation if we only want to
download the artifact for a module with a descriptor and not any dependencies. Or,
if we want to download another archive file, such as a TAR file, with documentation,
from a repository.

To use the artifact-only notation, we must add the file extension to the dependency
definition. If we use the string notation, we must add the extension prefixed with an
@ sign after the version. With the map notation, we can use the ext attribute to set
the extension. If we define our dependency as artifact-only, Gradle will not check
whether there is a module descriptor available for the dependency. In the next build
file, we will see examples of the different artifact-only notations:

```
dependencies {
    // Using the @ext notation to specify
    // we only want the artifact for this
    // dependency.
    vehicles 'com.vehicles:car:2.0@jar'

    // Use map notation with ext attribute
    // to specify artifact only dependency.
    traffic group: 'com.traffic', name: 'pedestrian',
        version: '1.0', ext: 'jar'

    // Alternatively we can use the configuration closure.
    // We need to specify an artifact configuration closure
    // as well to define the ext attribute.
    vehicles('com.vehicles:car:2.0') {
      artifact {
        name = 'car-docs'
        type = 'tar'
        extension = 'tar'
      }
    }
}
```

A Maven module descriptor can use classifiers for the artifact. This is mostly
used when a library with the same code is compiled for different Java versions,
for example, a library is compiled for Java 5 and Java 6 with the `jdk15` and `jdk16`
classifiers. We can use the `classifier` attribute when we define an external module
dependency to specify which classifier we want to use. Also, we can use it in a string
or map notation. With the string notation, we add an extra colon after the version
attribute and specify the classifier. For the map notation, we can add the `classifier`
attribute and specify the value we want. The following build file contains an example
of the different definitions of a dependency with a classifier:

```
dependencies {
  // Using string notation we can
  // append the classifier after
  // the version attribute, prefixed
  // with a colon.
  vehicles 'com.vehicles:car:2.0:jdk15'

  // With the map notation we simply use the
  // classifier attribute name and the value.
  traffic group: 'com.traffic', name: 'pedestrian',
      version: '1.0', classifier: 'jdk16'

  // Alternatively we can use the configuration closure.
  // We need to specify an artifact configuration closure
  // as well to define the classifier attribute.
  vehicles('com.vehicles:truck:2.0') {
    artifact {
      name = 'truck'
      type = 'jar'
      classifier = 'jdk15'
    }
  }
}
```

In the following section, we will see how we can define client module dependencies
in our build file.

Defining client module dependencies

When we define external module dependencies, we expect that there is a module
descriptor file with information about the artifacts and dependencies for those
artifacts. Gradle will parse this file and determine what needs to be downloaded.
Remember that if such a file is not available on the artifact, it will be downloaded.
However, what if we want to override the module descriptor or provide one if
it is not available? In the module descriptor that we provide, we can define the
dependencies of the module ourselves.

We can do this in Gradle with client module dependencies. Instead of relying on a module descriptor in a repository, we define our own module descriptor locally in the build file. We now have full control over what we think the module should look like and which dependencies the module itself has. We use the `module` method to define a client module dependency for a dependency configuration.

In the following example build file, we will write a client module dependency for the dependency car, and we will add a transitive dependency to the driver:

```
dependencies {
    // We use the module method to instruct
    // Gradle to not look for the module descriptor
    // in a repository, but use the one we have
    // defined in the build file.
    vehicles module('com.vehicles:car:2.0') {
        // Car depends on driver.
        dependency('com.traffic:driver:1.0')
    }
}
```

Using project dependencies

Projects can be part of a bigger, multi-project build, and the projects can be dependent on each other, for example, one project can be made dependent on the generated artifact of another project, including the transitive dependencies of the other project. To define such a dependency, we use the `project` method in our dependencies configuration block. We specify the name of the project as an argument. We can also define the name of a dependency configuration of the other project we depend on. By default, Gradle will look for the default dependency configuration, but with the `configuration` attribute, we can specify a specific dependency configuration to be used.

The next example build file will define project dependencies on the car and truck projects:

```
dependencies {
    // Use project method to define project
    // dependency on car project.
    vehicles project(':car')

    // Define project dependency on truck
    // and use dependency configuration api
    // from that project.
    vehicles project(':truck') {
```

```
    configuration = 'api'
  }

  // We can use alternative syntax
  // to specify a configuration.
  traffic project(path: ':pedestrian',
         configuration: 'lib')
}
```

Defining file dependencies

We can directly add files to a dependency configuration in Gradle. The files don't need to be stored in a repository but must be accessible from the project directory. Although most projects will have module descriptors stored in a repository, it is possible that a legacy project might have a dependency on files available on a shared network drive in the company. Otherwise, we must use a library in our project, which is simply not available in any repository. To add file dependencies to our dependency configuration, we specify a file collection with the `files` and `fileTree` methods. The following example build file shows the usage of all these methods:

```
dependencies {
  // Define a dependency on explicit file(s).
  vehicles files(
    'lib/vehicles/car-2.0.jar',
    'lib/vehicles/truck-1.0.jar'
  )

  // We can use the fileTree method to include
  // multiples from a directory and it's subdirectories.
  traffic fileTree(dir: 'deps', include: '*.jar')
}
```

The added files will not be part of the transitive dependencies of our project if we publish our project's artifacts to a repository, but they are if our project is part of a multi-project build.

Using internal Gradle and Groovy dependencies

When we write code to extend Gradle, such as custom tasks or plugins, we can have a dependency on the Gradle API and possibly the Groovy libraries used by the current Gradle version. We can use the `gradleApi` and `localGroovy` methods in our dependency configuration to have all the right dependencies.

If we are writing some Groovy code to extend Gradle, but we don't use any of the Gradle API classes, we can use `localGroovy`. With this method, the classes and libraries of the Groovy version shipped with the current Gradle version are added as dependencies. The following example build script uses the Groovy plugin and adds a dependency to the `compile` configuration on Groovy bundled with Gradle:

```
apply plugin: 'groovy'

dependencies {
    // Define dependency on Groovy
    // version shipped with Gradle.
    compile localGroovy()
}
```

When we write custom tasks or plugins for Gradle, we are dependent on the Gradle API. We need to import some of the API's classes in order to write our code. To define a dependency on the Gradle classes, we use the `gradleApi` method. This will include the dependencies for the Gradle version the build is executed for. The next example build file will show the use of this method:

```
apply plugin: 'groovy'

dependencies {
    // Define dependency on Gradle classes.
    compile gradleApi()
}
```

Using dynamic versions

Until now, we have set a version for a dependency explicitly with a complete version number. To set a minimum version number, we can use a special dynamic version syntax, for example, to set the dependency version to a minimum of 2.1 for a dependency, we use a version value of 2.1.+. Gradle will resolve the dependency to the latest version after version 2.1.0, or to version 2.1 itself. The upper bound is 2.2. In the following example, we will define a dependency on a spring-context version of at least 4.0.x:

```
dependencies {
    compile 'org.springframework:spring-context:4.0.+'
}
```

To reference the latest released version of a module, we can use `latest.integration` as the version value. We can also set the minimum and maximum version numbers we want. The following table shows the ranges we can use in Gradle:

Range	Description
`[1.0, 2.0]`	We can use all versions greater than or equal to 1.0 and lower than or equal to 2.0
`[1.0, 2.0[`	We can use all versions greater than or equal to 1.0 and lower than 2.0
`]1.0, 2.0]`	We can use all versions greater than 1.0 and lower than or equal to 2.0
`]1.0, 2.0[`	We can use all versions greater than 1.0 and lower than 2.0
`[1.0, )`	We can use all versions greater than or equal to 1.0
`]1.0, )`	We can use all versions greater than 1.0
`(, 2.0]`	We can use all versions lower than or equal to 2.0
`(, 2.0[`	We can use all versions lower than 2.0

In the following example build file, we will set the version for the spring-context module to greater than `4.0.1.RELEASE` and lower than `4.0.4.RELEASE`:

```
dependencies {
    // The dependency will resolve to version 4.0.3.RELEASE as
    // the latest version if available. Otherwise 4.0.2.RELEASE
    // or 4.0.1.RELEASE.
    compile 'org.springframework:spring-
    context:[4.0.1.RELEASE,4.0.4.RELEASE['
}
```

Getting information about dependencies

We have seen how we can define dependencies in our build scripts. To get more information about our dependencies, we can use the `dependencies` task. When we invoke the task, we can see which dependencies belong to the available configurations of our project. Also, any transitive dependencies are shown. The next example build file defines a dependency on Spring beans and we apply the Java plugin. We also specify a repository in the `repositories` configuration block. We will learn more about repositories in the next chapter. The following code captures the discussion in this paragraph:

```
apply plugin: 'java'

repositories {
    // Repository definition for JCenter Bintray.
    // Needed to download artifacts. Repository
```

```
      // definitions are covered later.
      jcenter()
  }

  dependencies {
    // Define dependency on spring-beans library.
    compile 'org.springframework:spring-beans:4.0.+'
  }
```

When we execute the dependencies task, we get the following output:

```
$ gradle -q dependencies


------------------------------------------------------------
Root project
------------------------------------------------------------


archives - Configuration for archive artifacts.
No dependencies

compile - Compile classpath for source set 'main'.
\--- org.springframework:spring-beans:4.0.+ -> 4.0.6.RELEASE
    \--- org.springframework:spring-core:4.0.6.RELEASE
        \--- commons-logging:commons-logging:1.1.3

default - Configuration for default artifacts.
\--- org.springframework:spring-beans:4.0.+ -> 4.0.6.RELEASE
    \--- org.springframework:spring-core:4.0.6.RELEASE
        \--- commons-logging:commons-logging:1.1.3

runtime - Runtime classpath for source set 'main'.
\--- org.springframework:spring-beans:4.0.+ -> 4.0.6.RELEASE
    \--- org.springframework:spring-core:4.0.6.RELEASE
        \--- commons-logging:commons-logging:1.1.3

testCompile - Compile classpath for source set 'test'.
\--- org.springframework:spring-beans:4.0.+ -> 4.0.6.RELEASE
    \--- org.springframework:spring-core:4.0.6.RELEASE
```

```
\--- commons-logging:commons-logging:1.1.3


testRuntime - Runtime classpath for source set 'test'.
\--- org.springframework:spring-beans:4.0.+ -> 4.0.6.RELEASE
    \--- org.springframework:spring-core:4.0.6.RELEASE
        \--- commons-logging:commons-logging:1.1.3
```

We see all the configurations of our project, and for each configuration, we see the defined dependency with the transitive dependencies. Also, we can see how our dynamic version `4.0.+` is resolved to version `4.0.6.RELEASE`. To only see dependencies for a specific configuration, we can use the `--configuration` option for the `dependencies` task. We must use the value of the configuration we want to see the dependencies for. In the following output, we see the result when we only want to see the dependencies for the compile configuration:

```
$ gradle -q dependencies --configuration compile


------------------------------------------------------------
Root project
------------------------------------------------------------


compile - Compile classpath for source set 'main'.
\--- org.springframework:spring-beans:4.0.+ -> 4.0.6.RELEASE
    \--- org.springframework:spring-core:4.0.6.RELEASE
        \--- commons-logging:commons-logging:1.1.3
```

There is also the `dependencyInsight` incubating task in Gradle. Because it is incubating, the functionality or syntax can change in future versions of Gradle. With the `dependencyInsight` task, we can find out why a specific dependency is in our build and to which configuration it belongs. We have to use the `--dependency` option, the required one, with part of the name of the dependency. Gradle will look for dependencies where the group, name, or version contains part of the specified value for the `--dependency` option. Optionally, we can specify the `--configuration` option to only look for the dependency in the specified configuration. If we leave out this option, Gradle will look for the dependency in all the configurations of our project.

Let's invoke the `dependencyInsight` task to find the dependencies with Spring in the name and in the runtime configuration:

```
$ gradle -q dependencyInsight --dependency spring --configuration runtime
org.springframework:spring-beans:4.0.6.RELEASE


org.springframework:spring-beans:4.0.+ -> 4.0.6.RELEASE
```

```
\--- runtime
```

```
org.springframework:spring-core:4.0.6.RELEASE
\--- org.springframework:spring-beans:4.0.6.RELEASE
     \--- runtime
```

In the output, we see how version 4.0.+ is resolved to 4.0.6.RELEASE. We also see that the spring-beans dependency and the transitive spring-core dependency are part of the runtime configuration.

Accessing dependencies

To access the configurations, we can use the configurations property of the Gradle project object. The configurations property contains a collection of Configuration objects. It is good to remember that a Configuration object is an instance of FileCollection. So, we can reference Configuration in our build scripts where FileCollection is allowed. The Configuration object contains more properties we can use to access the dependencies belonging to the configuration.

In the next example build, we will define two tasks that work with the files and information available from configurations in the project:

```
configurations {
  vehicles
  traffic.extendsFrom vehicles
}

task dependencyFiles << {
  // Loop through all files for the dependencies
  // for the traffic configuration, including
  // transitive dependencies.
  configurations.traffic.files.each { file ->
    println file.name
  }

  // We can also filter the files using
  // a closure. For example to only find the files
  // for dependencies with driver in the name.
  configurations.vehicles.files { dep ->
    if (dep.name.contains('driver')) {
      println dep.name
    }
  }

  // Get information about dependencies only belonging
```

```
    // to the vehicles configuration.
    configurations.vehicles.dependencies.each { dep ->
      println "${dep.group} / ${dep.name} / ${dep.version}"
    }

    // Get information about dependencies belonging
    // to the traffice configuration and
    // configurations it extends from.
    configurations.traffic.allDependencies.each {  dep ->
      println "${dep.group} / ${dep.name} / ${dep.version}"
    }
}

task copyDependencies(type: Copy) {
    description = 'Copy dependencies from configuration traffic to
    lib directory'

    // Configuration can be the source for a CopySpec.
    from configurations.traffic

    into "$buildDir/lib"
}
```

Buildscript dependencies

When we define dependencies, we mostly want to define them for the code we are developing. However, we may also want to add a dependency to the Gradle build script itself. We can write code in our build files, which might be dependent on a library that is not included in the Gradle distribution. Let's suppose we want to use a class from the Apache Commons Lang library in our build script. We must add a `buildscript` configuration closure to our build script. Within the configuration closure, we can define repositories and dependencies. We must use the special `classpath` configuration to add dependencies to. Any dependency added to the `classpath` configuration can be used by the code in our build file.

Let's see how this works with an example build file. We want to use the `org.apache.commons.lang3.RandomStringUtils` class inside a `randomString` task. This class can be found in the `org.apache.commons:commons-lang3` dependency. We define this as an external dependency for the `classpath` configuration. We also include a repository definition inside the `buildscript` configuration block so that the dependency can be downloaded. The following code shows this:

```
buildscript {
  repositories {
    // Bintray JCenter repository to download
    // dependency commons-lang3.
```

```
        jcenter()
    }

    dependencies {
        // Extend classpath of build script with
        // the classpath configuration.
        classpath 'org.apache.commons:commons-lang3:3.3.2'
    }
}

// We have add the commons-lang3 dependency
// as a build script dependency so we can
// reference classes for Apache Commons Lang.
import org.apache.commons.lang3.RandomStringUtils

task randomString << {
    // Use RandomStringUtils from Apache Commons Lang.
    String value = RandomStringUtils.randomAlphabetic(10)
    println value
}
```

To include external plugins, which are not part of the Gradle distribution, we can also use the classpath configuration in the buildscript configuration block. In the next example build file, we will include the Asciidoctor Gradle plugin:

```
buildscript {
    repositories {
        // We need the repository definition, from
        // where the dependency can be downloaded.
        jcenter()
    }

    dependencies {
        // Define external module dependency for the Gradle
        // Asciidoctor plugin.
        classpath 'org.asciidoctor:asciidoctor-gradle-plugin:0.7.3'
    }
}

// We defined the dependency on this external
// Gradle plugin in the buildscript {...}
// configuration block
apply plugin: 'org.asciidoctor.gradle.asciidoctor'
```

Optional Ant task dependencies

We can reuse the existing Ant tasks in Gradle. The default tasks from Ant can be invoked from within our build scripts. However, if we want to use an optional Ant task, we must define a dependency for the classes needed by the optional Ant task. We create a new dependency configuration, and then we add a dependency to this new configuration. We can reference this configuration when setting the classpath for the optional Ant task.

Let's add the optional Ant task SCP for the secure copying of files to/from a remote server. We create the `sshAntTask` configuration to add dependencies for the optional Ant task. We can choose any name for the configuration. To define the optional task, we use the `taskdef` method from the internal `ant` object. The method takes a `classpath` attribute, which must be the actual path of all files of the `sshAntTask` dependencies. The `Configuration` class provides the `asPath` property to return the path to the files in a platform-specific way. So, if we use this on a Windows computer, the file path separator is a `;` and for other platforms it is a `:`. The following example build file contains all the code to define and uses the SCP Ant task:

```
configurations {
    // We define a new dependency configuration.
    // This configuration is used to assign
    // dependencies to, that are needed by the
    // optional Ant task scp.
    sshAntTask
}

repositories {
    // Repository definition to download dependencies.
    jcenter()
}

dependencies {
    // Define external module dependencies
    // for the scp Ant task.
    sshAntTask(group: 'org.apache.ant',
        name: 'ant-jsch',
        version: '1.9.4')
}

// New task that used Ant scp task.
task copyRemote(
    description: 'Secure copy files to remote server') << {

    // Define optional Ant task scp.
```

```
ant.taskdef(
  name: 'scp',
  classname: 'org.apache.tools.ant.taskdefs.optional.ssh.Scp',

  // Set classpath based on dependencies assigned
  // to sshAntTask configuration. The asPath property
  // returns a platform-specific string value
  // with the dependency JAR files.
  classpath: configurations.sshAntTask.asPath)

// Invoke scp task we just defined.
ant.scp(
  todir: 'user@server:/home/user/upload',
  keyFile: '${user.home}/.ssh/id_rsa',
  passphrase: '***',
  verbose: true) {
  fileset(dir: 'html/files') {
    include name: '**/**'
  }
 }
}
```

Managing dependencies

You have already learned earlier in the chapter that we can refactor the dependency definitions by extracting common parts into project properties. This way, we only have to change a few project property values to make changes to multiple dependencies. In the next example build file, we will use lists to group dependencies together and reference those lists from the dependency definition:

```
ext {
  // Group is used multiple times, so
  // we extra the variable for re-use.
  def vehiclesGroup = 'com.vehicles'

  // libs will be available from within
  // the Gradle script code, like dependencies {...}.
  libs = [
    vehicles: [
      [group: vehiclesGroup, name: 'car', version: '2.0'],
      [group: vehiclesGroup, name: 'truck', version: '1.0']
    ],
    traffic: [
```

```
      [group: 'com.traffic', name: 'pedestrian', version:
      '1.0']
    ]
  ]
}

configurations {
  vehicles
}

dependencies {
  // Reference ext.libs.vehicles defined earlier
  // in the build script.
  vehicles libs.vehicles
}
```

Maven has a feature called dependency management metadata that allows us to define versions used for dependencies in a common part of the build file. Then, when the actual dependency is configured, we can leave out the version because it will be determined from the dependency management section of the build file. Gradle doesn't have such a built-in feature, but as illustrated earlier, we can use simple code refactoring to get a similar effect.

We can still have declarative dependency management, as we do in Maven, in our Gradle build, with the external dependency management plugin by Spring. This plugin adds a dependencyManagement configuration block to Gradle. Inside the configuration block, we can define dependency metadata, such as the group, name, and version. In the dependencies configuration closure in our Gradle build script, we don't have to specify the version anymore because it will be resolved via the dependency metadata in the dependencyManagement configuration. The following example build file uses this plugin and specifies dependency metadata using dependencyManagement:

```
buildscript {
  repositories {
    // Specific repository to find and download
    // dependency-management-plugin.
    maven {
      url 'http://repo.spring.io/plugins-snapshot'
    }
  }
  dependencies {
    // Define external module dependency with plugin.
    classpath 'io.spring.gradle:dependency-management-
    plugin:0.1.0.RELEASE'
```

```
    }
}

// Apply the external plugin dependency-management.
apply plugin: 'io.spring.dependency-management'
apply plugin: 'java'

repositories {
  // Repository for downloading dependencies.
  jcenter()
}

// This block is added by the dependency-management
// plugin to define dependency metadata.
dependencyManagement {
  dependencies {
    // Specify group:name followed by required version.
    'org.springframework.boot:spring-boot-starter-web'
    '1.1.5.RELEASE'

    // If we have multiple module names for the same group
    // and version we can use dependencySet.
    dependencySet(group: 'org.springframework.boot',
        version: '1.1.5.RELEASE') {
      entry 'spring-boot-starter-web'
      entry 'spring-boot-starter-actuator'
    }
  }
}

dependencies {
  // Version is resolved via dependencies metadata
  // defined in dependencyManagement.
  compile 'org.springframework.boot:spring-boot-starter-web'
}
```

To import a Maven **bill of materials (BOM)** provided by an organization, we can use the imports method inside the dependencyManagement configuration. In the next example, we will use the Spring IO platform BOM. In the dependencies configuration, we can leave out the version because it will be resolved via the BOM:

```
buildscript {
  repositories {
    // Specific repository to find and download
    // dependency-management-plugin.
```

```
      maven {
        url 'http://repo.spring.io/plugins-snapshot'
      }
    }
    dependencies {
      // Define external module dependency with plugin.
      classpath 'io.spring.gradle:dependency-management-
      plugin:0.1.0.RELEASE'
    }
}

// Apply the external plugin dependency-management.
apply plugin: 'io.spring.dependency-management'
apply plugin: 'java'

repositories {
  // Repository for downloading BOM and dependencies.
  jcenter()
}

// This block is added by the dependency-management
// plugin to define dependency metadata.
dependencyManagement {
  imports {
    // Use Maven BOM provided by Spring IO platform.
    mavenBom 'io.spring.platform:platform-bom:1.0.1.RELEASE'
  }
}

dependencies {
  // Version is resolved via Maven BOM.
  compile 'org.springframework.boot:spring-boot-starter-web'
}
```

Summary

In this chapter, you learned how to create and use dependency configurations to group together dependencies. We saw how to define several types of dependencies, such as external module dependency and internal dependencies.

Also, we saw how we can add dependencies to code in Gradle build scripts with the `classpath` configuration and the `buildscript` configuration.

Finally, we looked at some maintainable ways of defining dependencies using code refactoring and the external dependency management plugin.

In the next chapter, we will learn more about how we can configure repositories that store dependency modules.

2

Working with Repositories

In the previous chapter, you learned how to define dependencies for your project. Those dependencies are mostly stored somewhere in a repository or a directory structure. A repository usually has a structure to support different versions for the same dependency. Also, some metadata, such as the other dependencies for a module, is saved in the repository.

In our build files, we must define the location of a repository for our dependencies. We can mix different types of repositories, such as Maven and Ivy. We can even use a local filesystem as a repository. We will see how we can define and configure repositories in our build files.

Also, Gradle offers the option of configuring the repository layout, if the repository is using a custom layout. We will learn how to provide credentials for repositories with basic authentication.

Declaring repositories

If we want to add dependencies from a repository in a Gradle build file, we must explicitly add the `repositories` configuration block. Within the configuration block, we define the location of the repository and maybe some extra configuration. In the following example of a build file, we define a Maven repository with a custom location:

```
// Repositories configuration block,
// must be present to define and
// configure repositories to get
// dependencies in our build script.
repositories {

  // Sample Maven repository with a
  // custom location.
  maven {
```

```
    url 'http://mycompany.net/maven'
  }

}
```

We can include several repositories in our build file. We can even mix the type of repositories, for example to, include both the Ivy repository and a local filesystem. Gradle supports the following types of repositories:

Type	Description
Maven JCenter repository	This is a preconfigured repository for Bintray JCenter
Maven central repository	This is a preconfigured repository for Maven Central
Maven local repository	This is a preconfigured repository for the local Maven repository
Maven repository	This is a to-be-configured Maven repository, which has a custom location
Ivy repository	This is a to-be-configured Ivy repository, which has a location and layout
Flat directory repository	This is a local filesystem repository

We will see how to use these repositories in our build file later. It is good to realize that Gradle will try to download all artifacts from a dependency, from the same repository that the dependency module descriptor file is found. So, if we have multiple repositories defined in our build script, Gradle will still use the first repository that the module descriptor file is found on to download the artifacts.

Using the Maven JCenter repository

Bintray's JCenter is a relatively new public Maven repository, where a lot of Maven open source dependencies are stored. It is a superset of the Maven Central repository and also contains dependency artifacts published directly to JCenter. The URL to access the repository is `https://jcenter.bintray.com`. Gradle provides a shortcut for JCenter, so we don't have to type the URL ourselves in the `repositories` configuration block. The shortcut method is `jcenter()`.

In the following example build file, we define a reference to Bintray's JCenter repository using the `jcenter()` shortcut:

```
repositories {
  // Define Bintray's JCenter
  // repository, to find
  // dependencies.
  jcenter()
}
```

Since Gradle 2.1, the default protocol is `https` for the JCenter repository URL. If we want to use the `http` protocol, we must set the `url` property for the repository. In the next example build file, we will redefine the `url` property:

```
repositories {
  jcenter {
    // By default https is used as protocol,
    // but we can change it with the url
    // property.
    url = 'http://jcenter.bintray.com'
  }
}
```

Optionally, we can assign a name to the repository definition. This can be done for all Maven repositories, and because JCenter is also a Maven repository, we can set the `name` property. In the following example build file, we define multiple repositories and set the `name` property. We add a new task, `repositoriesInfo`, which will display the `name` and URL properties for each repository:

```
repositories {
  // Define multiple Maven repositories.
  jcenter()

  jcenter {
    name 'Bintray JCenter legacy'
    url = 'http://jcenter.bintray.com'
  }
}

task repositoriesInfo {
  description 'Display information about repositories'

  doFirst {
```

```
        // Access repositories as collection.
        project.repositories.each {
          // Display name and URL for each
          // repository.
          println "'${it.name}' uses URL ${it.url}"
        }
      }
    }
```

When we run the `repositoriesInfo` task, we get the following output:

```
$ gradle -q repositoriesInfo
'BintrayJCenter' uses URL https://jcenter.bintray.com/
'Bintray JCenter legacy' uses URL http://jcenter.bintray.com
```

Using the Maven Central repository

We can configure the central Maven 2 repository in the `repositories` configuration block. Gradle provides the shortcut method, `mavenCentral`. This configures the central Maven repository with the URL `https://repo1.maven.org/maven2/`.

In the next example build file, we will define the central Maven 2 repository for our build:

```
repositories {
  // Define central Maven repository
  // to use for dependencies.
  mavenCentral()
}
```

Gradle 2.1 uses the `https` protocol when we use the `mavenCentral` method. If we want to use the `http` protocol, we can redefine the `url` property and use the `http://repo1.maven.org/maven2/` address. In the next example build file, we will redefine the `url` property:

```
repositories {
  mavenCentral(
    // Use http protocol for the
    // central Maven repository.
    url: 'http://repo1.maven.org/maven2/'
  )
}
```

Besides changing the `url` property, we can also set an optional `name` property when we use the `mavenCentral` method. In the following example build script, we assign a value to the `name` property. We add a new task, `repositoriesInfo`, to display information about the configured repositories:

```
repositories {
  // Define multiple Maven repositories.
  mavenCentral()

  mavenCentral(
    name: 'HTTP Maven Central',
    url:  'http://repo1.maven.org/maven2/'
  )
}

task repositoriesInfo {
  description 'Display information about repositories'

  doFirst {
    // Access repositories as collection.
    project.repositories.each {
      // Display name and URL for each
      // repository.
      println "'${it.name}' uses URL ${it.url}"
    }
  }
}
```

Let's invoke the `repositoriesInfo` task to see the output:

```
$ gradle -q repositoriesInfo
'MavenRepo' uses URL https://repo1.maven.org/maven2/
'HTTP Maven Central' uses URL http://repo1.maven.org/maven2/
```

Using the Maven local repository

If we have used Maven on our local computer before there is a great change, we have a local Maven cache with downloaded artifacts. We can use this local cache as a repository in our Gradle build, with the `mavenLocal` shortcut method. Although it is possible to use our local Maven cache, it is not advisable because it makes the build dependent on local settings. If we work on a bigger project with more developers, then we cannot rely on the local Maven cache on each developer's computer as the only repository.

In the following example build file, we use the `mavenLocal` shortcut method:

```
repositories {
    // Define the local Maven cache as
    // a repository for dependencies.
    mavenLocal()
}
```

The location of the local Maven cache is determined in the same way as Maven. Gradle will try to find the `settings.xml` file in `USER_HOME/.m2` or `M2_HOME/conf`, where the former takes precedence over the latter. If the `settings.xml` file is found, then the location of the local Maven repository defined in the file is used. If `settings.xml` cannot be found, or if the local Maven repository location is not defined, then the default location is `USER_HOME/.m2/repository`.

Using Maven repositories

We have learned about shortcut methods to define a Maven repository. If we have our own Maven repository, such as Nexus or Artifactory, we can use the `maven` method in the `repositories` configuration block. With this method, we can define the `url` property to access the repository. We can see this in action in the following example build script:

```
repositories {

    // Define a custom Maven repository and
    // set the url property so Gradle can look
    // for the dependency module descripts
    // and artifacts.
    maven {
        url = 'http://ourcompany.com/maven'
        // Alternative syntax is to use
        // the url method:
        // url 'http://ourcompany.com/maven'
    }

}
```

When Gradle finds the module dependency descriptor in the Maven repository, then the artifacts will be searched for in this repository. If the artifacts are stored in another location, we use the `artifactUrls` property to specify the location. This way, Gradle will look for the dependency module descriptors in the location specified by the `url` property, and for the artifacts in the locations specified by the `artifactUrls` property.

The next example build script will define a custom Maven repository, with multiple locations for the artifacts:

```
repositories {
  maven {
    // At this location at the least the
    // dependency module descriptor files
    // must be stored.
    url 'http://ourcompany.com/maven'

    // Define extra locations where artifacts
    // can be found and downloaded.
    artifactUrls 'http://ourcompany.com/jars'
    artifactUrls 'http://ourcompany.com/lib'

    // Alternative syntax is to use the
    // artifactUrls property assignment:
    // artifactUrls = [
    //    'http://ourcompany.com/jars',
    'http://ourcompany.com/lib'
    // ]
  }
}
```

If we have configured our custom Maven repository with basic authentication, we must provide a username and password to access the repository. In our Gradle build file, we set the username and password in the `credentials` block of the `maven` configuration. Let's first add the username and password to the build file and later see how we can externalize these properties. The next example build file will use the `credentials` configuration block:

```
repositories {
  maven {
    url 'http://ourcompany.com/maven'

    // Here we assign the username and
    // password to access the repository.
    credentials {
      username = 'developer'
      password = 'secret'

      // Alternate syntax is to use
      // the username and password
      // methods.
      // username 'developer'
```

```
        // password 'secret'
      }
    }
  }
```

It is not a good idea to add the username and password to the build file, because this file is shared with all the developers involved in our project. We fix this using project properties, instead of a hardcoded username and password. The values of the project properties can be set via the command line with the -P or --project-prop options. Or, we can add the gradle.properties file to our project with the names and values of the project properties. The gradle.properties file must not be put in the version control system of our project, so that the values are private for the developer.

The following example build file uses the mavenUsername project properties and mavenPassword for the Maven repository credentials:

```
repositories {
  maven {
    name = 'Company Maven Repository'

    url 'http://ourcompany.com/maven'

    // Check that properties mavenUsername
    // and mavenPassword are set when
    // we run the script.
    verifyProperty('mavenUsername')
    verifyProperty('mavenPassword')

    credentials {
      // Use project properties instead
      // of hard coded username and password.
      username mavenUsername
      password mavenPassword
    }
  }
}

/**
 * Helper method to check if project property
 * with the given name is set.
 *
 * @param propertyName Name of the property to check
 * @throws GradleException When property is not set.
 */
void verifyProperty(final String propertyName) {
```

```
  if (!hasProperty(propertyName)) {
    throw new GradleException("Property $propertyName must be
    set")
  }
}
```

When we execute any tasks for this script, we should provide the values for the project properties via the command line:

```
$ gradle -PmavenUsername=developer -PmavenPassword=secret
```

Or, we can create the `gradle.properties` file in the project directory, with the following contents:

```
mavenUsername = developer
mavenPassword = secret
```

If we have multiple projects that use the same custom Maven repository, then we can also create a Gradle init script with the correct credentials. A Gradle init script runs before the build starts. In the script, we want to set the credentials for a Maven repository with a specific name. There are several ways to use an init script:

- We can use an init script directly from the command line with the `-I` or `--init-script` options. Here, we specify the name of the init script.

- We put the `init.gradle` file in the `USER_HOME/.gradle` directory. This file is run before every Gradle build on our computer.

- We put a file with the `.gradle` extension in the `USER_HOME/.gradle/init.d` directory. All Gradle init scripts from this directory are run before every build.

- We put a file with the `.gradle` extension in the `GRADLE_HOME/init.d` directory. This way, we can package a custom Gradle distribution with init scripts that always need to be executed.

Let's take a look at the contents of the init script in the next example init script file:

```
// Run for all projects.
allprojects {

  // After the project is evaluated, we can access
  // the repository by name.
  afterEvaluate { project ->

    // Check if project contains a repository
    // with the given name.
```

```
        if (project.repositories.any { it.name == 'Company Maven
        Repository' }) {

            // Set credentials for custom Maven repository
            // with the given name.
            configure(project.repositories['Company Maven
            Repository']) {
                credentials {
                    username 'developer'
                    password 'secret'
                }
            }

        }

    }

}
```

We must change our project Gradle build file, because the credentials are now set via an init script. We will remove the credentials from the project build file. In the next example build file, we will remove the credentials and helper method, to set the credential properties. The credentials are set by the init script. The following code shows this:

```
repositories {
  maven {
    name = 'Company Maven Repository'
    url 'http://ourcompany.com/maven'

    // Credentials are set via init script.
  }
}
```

Using the flat directory repository

Gradle also allows directories to be used as repositories to solve dependencies. We can specify one or more directories using the flatDir method. Optionally, we can specify a name for the repository. In the next example build file, we specify the lib and jars directories to be used as repositories:

```
repositories {

    // Define the directories jars and lib
    // to be used as repositories.
```

```
flatDir {
  name 'Local lib directory'
  dirs "${projectDir}/jars", "${projectDir}/lib"
}

// Alternate syntax is using a Map
// with the flatDir method.
// flatDir name: 'Local lib directory',
//         dirs: ["${projectDir}/jars", "${projectDir}/lib"]

}
```

When we use the flat directory repository, Gradle resolves dependency artifacts based on the artifact name and version. The group part of a dependency is ignored. If we only use flat directory repositories in our project, we can even leave out the group part when we configure the dependencies. Gradle uses the following rules to resolve a dependency:

- [artifact]-[version].[ext]
- [artifact]-[version]-[classifier].[ext]
- [artifact].[ext]
- [artifact]-[classifier].[ext]

In the next example build file, we will define a flat directory repository and a single dependency:

```
repositories {
  flatDir name: 'Local lib directory',
      dirs: ["${projectDir}/lib"]
}

dependencies {
  traffic group: 'com.traffic', name: 'pedestrian',
      version: '1.0', classifier: 'jdk16'
}
```

Gradle will resolve the following files in the lib directory; the first matching file is used:

- pedestrian-1.0.jar
- pedestrian-1.0-jdk16.jar
- pedestrian.jar
- pedestrian-jdk16.jar

Using Ivy repositories

Ivy repositories allow customizable and flexible repository layout patterns. Gradle supports Ivy repositories, and we can configure the repository layout patterns in our Gradle build script. To define an Ivy repository, we use the `ivy` method in the `repositories` configuration block.

In the following example build file, we define a standard Ivy repository, and we also set the optional `name` property for the repository:

```
repositories {

  // Define an Ivy repository with
  // a URL and optional name property.
  ivy {
    name 'Ivy Repository'
    url 'http://ourompany.com/repo'
  }

}
```

The layout of an Ivy repository defines the patterns used to search module dependency metadata and the dependency artifacts. We can use some predefined layouts in our build scripts. In the previous example build file, we didn't specify a layout. Gradle will then use the default `gradle` layout. The next table shows the different layout names we can use, their patterns to find the Ivy metadata XML files, and the artifacts for the dependency:

Name	Ivy pattern	Artifact pattern
gradle	[organisation]/ [module]/[revision]/ ivy-[revision].xml	[organisation]/[module]/ [revision]/[artifact]- [revision](-[classifier]) (.[ext])
maven	[organisation]/ [module]/[revision]/ ivy-[revision].xml	[organisation]/[module]/ [revision]/[artifact]- [revision](-[classifier]) (.[ext])
ivy	[organisation]/[module]/ [revision]/[type]s/ [artifact](.[ext])	[organisation]/[module]/ [revision]/[type]s/[artifact] (.[ext])

The `.` in `organisation` is replaced with `/`.

To use a layout, we use the `layout` method inside the `ivy` configuration. For example, in the next build script, we use the `maven` and `ivy` layouts:

```
repositories {

  ivy {
    // Set layout to maven.
    layout 'maven'
    name 'Ivy repository Maven layout'
    url 'http://ourcompany.com/repo1'
  }

  ivy {
    // Set layout to ivy.
    layout 'ivy'
    name 'Ivy repository'
    url 'http://ourcompany.com/repo'
  }

}
```

To define a custom pattern for the Ivy XML files and the artifacts, we use the `pattern` layout. With this layout, we define our own patterns using the tokens defined by Ivy. In the following table, we see the tokens that can be used to build a pattern:

Token	Description
[organisation]	This is the organisation name.
[orgPath]	This is the organisation name, where . has been replaced by /. This can be used to configure maven2-like repositories.
[module]	This is the module name.
[branch]	This is the branch name.
[revision]	This is the revision name.
[artifact]	This is the artifact name (or ID).
[type]	This is the artifact type.
[ext]	This is the artifact file extension.
[conf]	This is the configuration name.
[originalname]	This is the original artifact name (including the extension).

To specify an optional token, we enclose the token with parentheses ((and)). If the token defined between parentheses is null or empty, then the token is ignored. For example, the `[artifact](-[revision]).[ext]` pattern will accept `artifact.jar` if revision is not set and `artifact-1.1.jar` if revision is set.

We define a custom layout in our build script by specifying the layout with the `pattern` name, and adding a configuration block where we define the patterns for the Ivy XML files and artifacts. If we don't specify a special pattern for the Ivy XML files, then the artifact pattern is used. We need to define at least one artifact pattern. The patterns are appended to the `url` property of the repository. Optionally, we can set the `pattern` layout property, `m2compatible`. If the value is `true`, then the . in the `[organisation]` token is replaced with /.

In the next example build script, we will define two new repositories with a custom layout:

```
repositories {

  ivy {
    url 'http://ourcompany.com/repo'

    // Here we define a custom pattern
    // for the artifacts and Ivy XML files.
    layout('pattern') {
      // Define pattern with artifact method.
      // This pattern is used for both Ivy XML files
      // and artifacts.
      artifact '[module]/[type]/[artifact]-[revision].[ext]'
    }
  }

  ivy {
    url 'http://ourcompany.com/repo1'

    layout('pattern') {
      // We can define multiple patterns.
      // The order of the definitions
      // defines search path.
      artifact 'binaries/[organisation]/[module]/[artifact]-
[revision].[ext]'
      artifact 'signed-
jars/[organisation]/[module]/[artifact]-[revision].[ext]'

      // Seperate definition for Ivy XML files
      // with ivy method.
      ivy '[organisation]/[module]/metadata/ivy-
[revision].xml'
    }
  }

}
```

An alternative syntax to define custom patterns is using `artifactPattern` and `ivyPattern` inside the `ivy` configuration block. We don't have to use the `layout` method with this definition. If we don't specify `ivyPattern`, then the pattern defined with `artifactPattern` is used to find Ivy XML files. In the following example build script, we rewrite the repository definitions from the previous example build file:

```
repositories {

  ivy {
    url 'http://ourcompany.com/repo'

    // Define pattern with artifact method.
    // This pattern is used for both Ivy XML files
    // and artifacts.
    artifactPattern '[module]/[type]/[artifact]-
    [revision].[ext]'
  }

  ivy {
    url 'http://ourcompany.com/repo1'

    // We can define multiple patterns. The order of the
    definitions
    // defines search path.
    artifactPattern
    'binaries/[organisation]/[module]/[artifact]-[revision].[ext]'
    artifactPattern 'signed-
    jars/[organisation]/[module]/[artifact]-[revision].[ext]'

    // Seperate definition for Ivy XML files with ivy method.
    ivyPattern '[organisation]/[module]/metadata/ivy-
    [revision].xml'
  }

}
```

To specify the username and password for an Ivy repository with basic authentication, we use the `credentials` method, just as we did with the Maven repositories. In the next example build file, we will set the credentials to access an Ivy repository. Take a look at the section about Maven repositories to see how we can externalize the username and password, so that they are not part of the build script code. The following code shows this:

```
repositories {
  ivy {
```

```
url 'http://ourcompany.com/repo'

// Here we assign the username and
// password to access the repository.
credentials {
  username = 'developer'
  password = 'secret'

  // Alternate syntax is to use
  // the username and password
  // methods.
  // username 'developer'
  // password 'secret'
  }
 }
}
```

Using different protocols

The Maven and Ivy repositories can be accessed via several protocols. We already learned that we can use the http and https protocols. However, we can also use the file and sftp protocols. We must provide credentials when we use the sftp protocol. The file protocol doesn't support authentication.

The next example build file will use the file and sftp protocols to define the Maven and Ivy repositories:

```
repositories {
  ivy {
    // Use file protocol, for example an
    // accessible network share or local directory.
    url 'file://Volumes/shared/developers/repo'
  }

  maven {
    url 'sftp://ourcompany.com:22/repo'

    // With the sftp protocol we must provide
    // the username and password.
    credentials {
      username 'developer'
      password 'secret'
    }
  }
}
```

Summary

In this chapter, you learned how to define repositories in your Gradle build scripts. You saw how to use predefined shortcut methods: `jcenter`, `mavenCentral`, and `mavenLocal`. To access a Maven repository at a custom location, we can use the `url` property and the `maven` method. When we configure an Ivy repository, we have the most control. We can specify a URL, and also the layout pattern of the repository. You learned that you can also use a flat directory repository in your build scripts.

You saw how to provide credentials for repositories with basic authentication. You now know how to save the username and password outside your build script. Finally, you learned how to use different transport protocols to access repositories.

In the next chapter, we will see how Gradle will resolve dependencies.

3
Resolving Dependencies

In *Chapter 1, Defining Dependencies*, you learned how to add dependencies to your projects. We have seen different ways of specifying dependencies, such as module or project dependencies. In the previous chapter, we explored how to define the repositories that host our dependencies. Gradle will use this information to do the actual dependency resolution. In this chapter, we will see how Gradle resolves dependencies.

Gradle has a different way of resolving version conflicts than other build tools, so we will take a good look at what happens when a dependency is resolved. We will see how we can customize the resolution process in Gradle so that we can have the exact dependencies we want and have reliable and repeatable builds.

Understanding dependency resolution

Gradle will use the information in the `repositories` and `dependencies` configuration blocks to gather and download all dependencies. This process is also called **dependency resolution**. The following steps are taken by Gradle to resolve dependencies:

1. The module descriptor file for a dependency is searched in the defined repositories. The order of the repository definitions is used for searching. So, repositories defined before other repositories are searched first, and so on. If a POM or Ivy descriptor file is found, it is used. If no descriptor file is found, then the artifact file for the dependency is searched. If either the descriptor file or the artifact file is found, then Gradle knows this repository can be used to download the dependencies.

    ° If a POM descriptor file is found with a parent POM descriptor file, then the parent POM is resolved by Gradle.

- ○ A dynamic version, like *4.1.+*, is resolved to the highest available static version in the repository. For example if the repository contains versions *4.1.0* and *4.1.1* then the *4.1.1* version is used.

2. Gradle will determine which repository is the best to use based on the following criteria:
   - ○ Module descriptor files, like POM and Ivy descriptor files, are preferred over artifact file only.
   - ○ Dependencies found in earlier repositories are preferred over later repositories.
   - ○ If a dynamic version like 2.+ is used, than a higher static version is preferred over a lower static version.

3. The artifacts for the module dependency are downloaded from the repository that is chosen by Gradle. This means that artifacts are not downloaded from a different repository than where the descriptor file or artifact file for the defined dependency are found.

If a dependency is defined with a static version, and Gradle finds a module descriptor file for this dependency in a repository, then the search for this dependency is complete, and other repositories will not be used for the search. The process cannot come up with a better repository candidate, so the dependency resolution is finished for the dependency.

Configuring transitive dependencies

Most of the time dependencies in our project are also dependent on other libraries. So, the dependencies have dependencies of their own. These are so-called transitive dependencies. Gradle must be able to resolve the transitive dependencies as well.

In the following example build file, we define the `logback-classic` module dependency with the version 1.1.2 and the group name `ch.qos.logback`:

```
apply plugin: 'java'

repositories.jcenter()

dependencies {
  // Dependency definition for Logback classic
  // library, used as implementation for SLF4J API.
  compile 'ch.qos.logback:logback-classic:1.1.2'
}
```

When we run the Gradle `dependencies` task, we can see that our defined dependency for `logback-classic` depends on `ch.qos.logback:logback-core:1.1.2` and `org.slf4j:slf4j-api:1.7.6`. The following code shows this:

```
$ gradle -q dependencies --configuration compile
---------------------------------------------------------
Root project
---------------------------------------------------------


compile - Compile classpath for source set 'main'.
\--- ch.qos.logback:logback-classic:1.1.2
  +--- ch.qos.logback:logback-core:1.1.2
  \--- org.slf4j:slf4j-api:1.7.6
```

Disabling transitive dependencies

If we don't want to have transitive dependencies in our project, we must reconfigure the dependency or configuration. With Gradle, we have different ways to disable transitive behavior for dependencies. First, we can add a configuration closure to our dependency definition, use the `transitive` property, and set the value to `false`. By default, all dependencies are treated as transitive, as we saw in our example build file.

In the following example build file, we specify that we want to treat or use the `logback-classic` dependency as nontransitive:

```
apply plugin: 'java'

repositories.jcenter()

dependencies {
  // Dependency definition for Logback classic.
  compile 'ch.qos.logback:logback-classic:1.1.2', {
    // We don't want to have the transitive dependencies.
    transitive = false
  }
}
```

If we run the `dependencies` task again, we can see in the output that the transitive dependencies are no longer resolved:

```
$ gradle -q dependencies --configuration compile


------------------------------------------------------------
Root project
------------------------------------------------------------


compile - Compile classpath for source set 'main'.
\--- ch.qos.logback:logback-classic:1.1.2
```

We can also disable transitive dependencies for a dependency configuration as a whole. So, this means that any dependencies defined with the configuration will not have transitive dependencies. Single dependencies within the configuration can use the `transitive` property in the configuration closure to enable transitive behavior again for that dependency. To accomplish this, perform the following steps:

1. First, we will disable transitive dependencies for the `compile` configuration in the next example build file:

```
apply plugin: 'java'

repositories.jcenter()

configurations {
   // Disable transitive dependencies for
   // all dependencies defined in this
   // configuration.
   // Configurations extended
   // from the compile configuration will not
   // inherit this transitive property value.
   compile.transitive = false
}

dependencies {
   // Dependency definition for Logback classic
   compile 'ch.qos.logback:logback-classic:1.1.2'
}
```

2. Next, we will execute the `dependencies` task and see that transitive dependencies are no longer resolved:

```
$ gradle -q dependencies --configuration compile

------------------------------------------------------------
Root project
------------------------------------------------------------

compile - Compile classpath for source set 'main'.
\--- ch.qos.logback:logback-classic:1.1.2
```

Excluding transitive dependencies

We can also have more fine-grained control of transitive dependencies. We can exclude certain transitive dependencies in our dependency definition. This way, we can choose to use only certain transitive dependencies and leave others out. To define which transitive dependencies we want to exclude, we use the `exclude` method in the configuration closure of our dependency.

Let's see how we can include the `logback-core` transitive dependency but remove the `slf4j-api` dependency. We use the `exclude` method in the configuration closure. The `exclude` method takes `Map` as an argument with one or both of the keys: `module` and `group`. In the following build file, we include the `logback-core` transitive dependency:

```
apply plugin: 'java'

repositories.jcenter()

dependencies {
  // Dependency definition for Logback classic
  compile('ch.qos.logback:logback-classic:1.1.2') {
    // Exclude slf4j-api transitive dependency.
    exclude module: 'slf4j-api'
    // Alternative syntax:
    // Exclude all modules in the group org.slf4j:
    // exclude group: 'org.slf4j'
    // Or specify both group and module name:
    // exclude group: 'org.slf4j', module: 'slf4j-api'
  }
}
```

We execute the `dependencies` task to see whether our configuration definition has the desired effect:

```
$ gradle -q dependencies --configuration compile


------------------------------------------------------------

Root project

------------------------------------------------------------


compile - Compile classpath for source set 'main'.
\--- ch.qos.logback:logback-classic:1.1.2
   \--- ch.qos.logback:logback-core:1.1.2
```

Notice that in the output, the transitive dependency, `org.slf4j:slf4j-api:1.7.6`, is no longer part of our transitive dependencies.

We can also set exclude rules on a configuration in addition to a single dependency. The exclude rule on a configuration will be used for all dependencies defined within the configuration. In the next example Gradle build file, we will exclude the `slf4j-api` module from all dependencies in the `compile` configuration:

```
apply plugin: 'java'

repositories.jcenter()

configurations {
  compile {
    // Exclude slf4j-api transitive dependency.
    exclude module: 'slf4j-api'
    // Alternative syntax:
    // Exclude all modules in the group org.slf4j:
    // exclude group: 'org.slf4j'
    // Or specify both group and module name:
    // exclude group: 'org.slf4j', module: 'slf4j-api'
  }

  // To exclude a module and/or group from all configurations
  // we can use the all method:
  // all { exclude module: 'slf4j-api' }
}

dependencies {
  // Dependency definition for Logback classic.
  compile('ch.qos.logback:logback-classic:1.1.2')
}
```

Any exclude rule that we add to either the configuration or the dependency is accessible again via the `excludeRules` property of the corresponding objects. We can use this to find out the configuration or dependency that is responsible for excluding a certain dependency. In the following example build file, we create a new task, `showExcludeRules`, where we loop through all configurations and dependencies and collect exclude rules. At the end of the task, we print all the information to standard output. The following code shows this:

```
apply plugin: 'java'

repositories.jcenter()

configurations {
  compile {
    exclude module: 'slf4j-api'
  }
}

dependencies {
  compile('ch.qos.logback:logback-classic:1.1.2') {
    exclude group: 'ch.qos.logback', module: 'logback-core'
  }
}

task showExcludeRules {
  description 'Show exclude rules for configurations and
  dependencies'

  doFirst {
    // Store found exclude rules.
    def excludes = []

    // Go through all configurations to find exclude rules
    // defined at configuration level and at
    // dependency level for dependencies in the configuration.
    configurations.all.each { configuration ->
      def configurationExcludes = configuration.excludeRules
      configurationExcludes.findAll().each { rule ->
        // Add found excludeRule to excludes collection.
        excludes << [type: 'container',
              id: configuration.name,
              excludes: rule]
      }

      def dependencies = configuration.allDependencies
```

```
        dependencies.all { dependency ->
          def excludeRules = dependency.excludeRules

          excludeRules.findAll().each { rule ->
            def dep = dependency
            def id = "${dep.group}:${dep.name}:${dep.version}"
            // Add found excludeRule to excludes collection.
            excludes << [type: 'dependency', id: id, excludes: rule]
          }
        }
      }

      // Printing exclude rule information for output.
      def printExcludeRule = {
        def rule = "${it.excludes.group ?:
        '*'}:${it.excludes.module ?: '*'}"
        println "$it.id >> $rule"
      }

      // Print formatted header for output.
      def printHeader = { header ->
        println()
        println '-' * 60
        println header
        println '-' * 60
      }

      // Group rules by organisation or dependency.
      def excludeRules = excludes.groupBy { it.type }

      printHeader 'Configurations'
      excludeRules.container.toSet().each(printExcludeRule)

      printHeader 'Dependencies'
      excludeRules.dependency.toSet().each(printExcludeRule)
    }
  }
```

When we run the task, we get the following output:

```
$ gradle -q showExcludeRules


------------------------------------------------------------

Configurations
```

```
------------------------------------------------------------
compile >> *:slf4j-api


------------------------------------------------------------
Dependencies
------------------------------------------------------------
ch.qos.logback:logback-classic:1.1.2 >> ch.qos.logback:logback-core
```

Using artifact-only dependencies

Finally, we can use the `ext` attribute for an external module dependency if we know we only want to include a single artifact from the dependency. With this attribute, no transitive dependencies are resolved because we specify that we specifically want the artifact specified by the `ext` attribute.

In our example, we can use the `ext` attribute with the `jar` value to resolve only the JAR artifact for the `logback-classic` dependency. In the next example build file, we will use the `ext` attribute for our `logback-classic` dependency:

```
apply plugin: 'java'

repositories.jcenter()

dependencies {
  // Dependency definition for Logback classic library
  compile 'ch.qos.logback:logback-classic:1.1.2@jar'

  // Alternative syntax:
  //compile group: 'ch.qos.logback',
  //        name: 'logback-classic',
  //        version: '1.1.2',
  //        ext: 'jar'
}
```

Resolving version conflicts

Our previous examples were simple and only contained one dependency with some transitive dependencies. When we add more dependencies to our project, or have a multimodule project where each project has a lot of dependencies, then it can happen that the same dependency or transitive dependency is included multiple times. Gradle detects this and makes sure that the dependency is only downloaded once. We will see more about the advanced dependency cache management in Gradle later.

The trouble begins when the same dependency is included multiple times but with different versions. Which version of the dependency should be used? This is where Gradle's resolution strategy comes into play. The next table shows the resolution strategies that Gradle has:

Name	Description
Newest	The newest version of a conflicting dependency is used. This is the default strategy used by Gradle. If the versions of the conflicting dependency are backward compatible, this works fine.
Fail	The build process fails when there is a version conflict with dependencies. We must explicitly add code to our build file that will resolve the version conflict. We will see later in this chapter how we can customize the resolution strategy to solve version conflicts explicitly.

Using the newest version

Let's see what happens if we have a version conflict and use the default resolution strategy of Gradle. Gradle will use the newest version of the dependency that has a version conflict. To accomplish this, perform the following steps:

1. In the next build file, we define a dependency on `slf4j-api` in the `compile` configuration and on `logback-classic` in the `runtime` configuration:

```
apply plugin: 'java'

repositories.jcenter()

dependencies {
  // Define dependency on SLF4J API for
  // compiling source files.
  compile 'org.slf4j:slf4j-api:1.7.7'

  // Define implementation Logback classic
  // of SLF4J API in runtime configuration.
  // This has a transitive dependency on
  // org.slf4j:slf4j-api:1.7.6, which is a version
  // conflict with org.slf4j:slf4j-api:1.7.7
  runtime 'ch.qos.logback:logback-classic:1.1.2'
}
```

2. We run the `dependencies` task to see which versions of the dependencies are used. The following output shows that the `org.slf4j:slf4j-api:1.7.6` transitive dependency of `logback-classic` is changed, so the version `1.7.7` is used, which is defined in the `compile` configuration:

```
$ gradle -q dependencies --configuration runtime


------------------------------------------------------------

Root project

------------------------------------------------------------


runtime - Runtime classpath for source set 'main'.
+--- org.slf4j:slf4j-api:1.7.7
\--- ch.qos.logback:logback-classic:1.1.2
     +--- ch.qos.logback:logback-core:1.1.2
     \--- org.slf4j:slf4j-api:1.7.6 -> 1.7.7


(*) - dependencies omitted (listed previously)
```

Notice the line `org.slf4j:slf4j-api:1.7.6 → 1.7.7`, where it visually shows that the version is increased for this dependency from `1.7.6` to `1.7.7`.

3. The `dependencies` task shows a hierarchical tree view of the dependencies and transitive dependencies. To get a view from a specific dependency, and to see how it got in the dependency graph, we use the `dependencyInsight` task. With this task, we can see how the dependency is resolved and whether any conflict resolution has happened.

4. We must use the following two options when we invoke the `dependencyInsight` task from the command line:

    1. We specify the configuration of the dependency with the `--configuration` option.
    2. Then, we use the `--dependency` option to specify the name of the dependency.

5. The name of the dependency doesn't have to be the full name; we can even use part of the name. For example, we can use `org.slf4j:slf4j-api`, `slf4j-api`, and `slf4j` to gain insight into a dependency.

6. We execute the `dependencyInsight` task to see more information about the `slf4j-api` dependency in our example build file:

```
$ gradle -q dependencyInsight --configuration runtime --dependency
slf4j-api
org.slf4j:slf4j-api:1.7.7 (conflict resolution)
\--- runtime


org.slf4j:slf4j-api:1.7.6 -> 1.7.7
\--- ch.qos.logback:logback-classic:1.1.2
    \--- runtime
```

In the output, we see that the `org.slf4j:slf4j-api:1.7.7` dependency is resolved for the `runtime` configuration and that conflict resolution has happened for the dependency. In the next lines, we will see that the `org.slf4j:slf4j-api:1.7.6` transitive dependency has its version increased from `1.7.6` to `1.7.7`. The `dependencyInsight` task already tells us more about the dependency resolution that is applied. We will probably start with a broad overview using the `dependencies` task, and if we want to get more information about a particular dependency, we will use the `dependencyInsight` task.

7. There is another task that we can use that will combine both the `dependencies` and `dependencyInsight` tasks. The `htmlDependencyReport` task is part of the `project-report` plugin. With this task, we get an HTML report showing all dependencies, and we can click on dependencies to get more insight. To use the task, we first add the `project-report` plugin to our example project file. The following code shows this:

```
apply plugin: 'java'
apply plugin: 'project-report'

repositories.jcenter()

dependencies {
  compile 'org.slf4j:slf4j-api:1.7.7'

  runtime 'ch.qos.logback:logback-classic:1.1.2'
}
```

8. We execute the `htmlDependencyReport` task for this build file. The following code shows this:

```
$ gradle htmlDependencyReport
:htmlDependencyReport

BUILD SUCCESSFUL

Total time: 1.645 secs
$
```

9. After the task is executed, new files are created in `build/reports/project/dependencies/`.

10. When we open the `index.html` file in a web browser, we can see the name of our project. If we had a multimodule project, we would see all project names here. We can click on the name and get an overview of all configurations. In the next screenshot, we see an overview of all the configuration in our project:

11. When we click on the `runtime` configuration link, all dependencies are shown. We can see that there is a version conflict because the `org.sfl4j:slf4j-api:1.7.6` dependency is orange in color. This view is what we also see when the dependencies task from the command line is invoked:

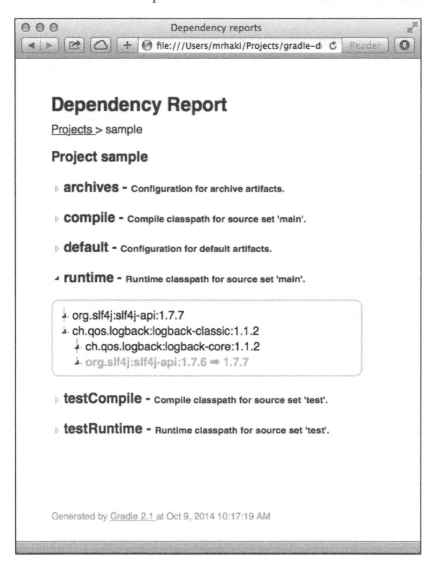

12. To get the dependency insight view, we click on the `org.sfl4j:slf4j-api:1.7.6` → `1.7.7` link. A pop-up window is opened in our web browser, and we see the following screenshot:

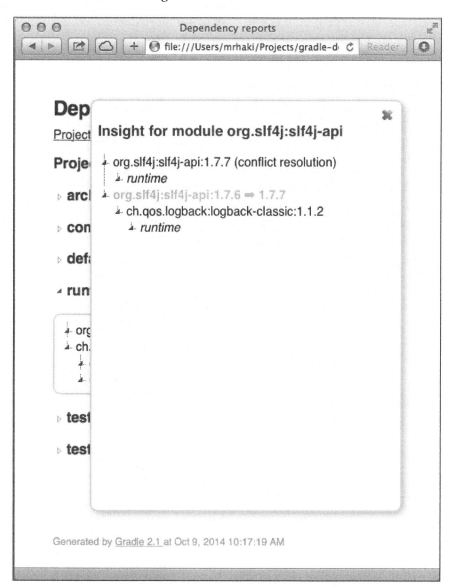

Now, we see what we normally see if we run the `dependencyInsight` task from the command line.

The `htmlDependencyReport` is very useful to get a graphical and interactive view of the dependencies in our project. It is also easy to get more details about a dependency by just clicking on it in the generated HTML reports.

Failing on version conflict

If the default Gradle resolution strategy of using the newest version of a (transitive) dependency is not solving the problem, we can choose to let the build fail if there is a version conflict. To run the build successfully again, we must explicitly solve the version conflict in our build file.

In the following example build file, we configure the resolution strategy for the `runtime` configuration to fail if there is a version conflict. The `resolutionStrategy` method accepts a configuration closure where we invoke the `failOnVersionConflict` method. The following code shows this:

```
apply plugin: 'java'

repositories.jcenter()

configurations {
  runtime {
    resolutionStrategy {
      // If there is a version conflict,
      // then the build must fail.
      failOnVersionConflict()
    }
  }

  // Alternatively we could apply
  // this to all configurations:
  // all {
  //      resolutionStrategy {
  //          failOnVersionConflict()
  //      }
  // }
}

dependencies {
  compile 'org.slf4j:slf4j-api:1.7.7'

  runtime 'ch.qos.logback:logback-classic:1.1.2'
}
```

The build is now configured to fail on a version conflict. We know from the previous examples in this chapter that there is a version conflict on `slf4j-api`. We now execute the `dependencies` task to see what happens:

```
$ gradle -q dependencies


------------------------------------------------------------

Root project

------------------------------------------------------------


runtime - Runtime classpath for source set 'main'.


FAILURE: Build failed with an exception.


* What went wrong:
Execution failed for task ':dependencies'.
> Could not resolve all dependencies for configuration ':runtime'.
   > A conflict was found between the following modules:
        - org.slf4j:slf4j-api:1.7.7
        - org.slf4j:slf4j-api:1.7.6


* Try:
Run with --stacktrace option to get the stack trace. Run with --info or
--debug option to get more log output.
```

We see that the build has failed this time. In the output, we see why. There is a conflict between the `org.slf4j:slf4j-api:1.7.7` and `org.slf4j:slf4j-api:1.7.6` modules.

Forcing a version

We can force Gradle to use a specific version for a dependency in our project. The dependency can also be transitive. We use the configuration closure for a dependency and set the `force` property with the value `true`. This instructs the Gradle dependency resolution process to always use the specified version for this dependency, even when the dependency is a transitive dependency in the dependency graph.

In our example build file, we have a version conflict. We can fix this by forcing Gradle to use the version 1.7.7 for the org.slf4j:slf4j-api dependency. The following example build file applies the force property:

```
apply plugin: 'java'

repositories.jcenter()

configurations {
  runtime {
    resolutionStrategy {
      failOnVersionConflict()
    }
  }
}

dependencies {
  compile 'org.slf4j:slf4j-api:1.7.7', {
    // Force Gradle to use this version
    // for this dependency (even transtive).
    force = true
  }

  runtime 'ch.qos.logback:logback-classic:1.1.2'
}
```

Let's run the dependencies task to see whether the version conflict is now resolved:

```
$ gradle -q dependencies --configuration runtime


------------------------------------------------------------
Root project
------------------------------------------------------------


runtime - Runtime classpath for source set 'main'.
+--- org.slf4j:slf4j-api:1.7.7
\--- ch.qos.logback:logback-classic:1.1.2
     +--- ch.qos.logback:logback-core:1.1.2
     \--- org.slf4j:slf4j-api:1.7.6 -> 1.7.7


(*) - dependencies omitted (listed previously)
```

We have resolved the version conflict, and the build is now successful again. We can also see in the output that for the `org.slf4j:slf4j-api:1.7.6` transitive dependency, the version is now the version `1.7.7`.

Instead of setting the `force` property in the dependency configuration, we can also force a version for a dependency as part of the `resolutionStrategy` method in the `configurations` configuration block. We use the `force` method to add a dependency with a forced version. Alternatively, we can use the `forcedModules` property to define all forced dependencies. This might be a better solution because we can have multiple dependencies with a forced version and put them all together in the `resolutionStrategy` configuration closure for a more readable and maintainable build file.

In the next example build file, we will force the version of the `org.slf4j:slf4j-api` dependency to be `1.7.7`, but this time as part of the `resolutionStrategy` configuration:

```
apply plugin: 'java'

repositories.jcenter()

configurations {
  runtime {
    resolutionStrategy {
      failOnVersionConflict()

      // Make sure version 1.7.7 is used for
      // (transitive) dependency org.slf4j:slf4j-api.
      force 'org.slf4j:slf4j-api:1.7.7'

      // Alternate syntax is to define the
      // forced module collection.
      // forcedModules = ['org.slf4j:slf4j-api:1.7.7']
    }
  }
}

dependencies {
  compile 'org.slf4j:slf4j-api:1.7.7'

  runtime 'ch.qos.logback:logback-classic:1.1.2'
}
```

When we execute the `dependencies` task from the command line, we see that the version `1.7.7` is used for all `org.slf4j:slf4j-api` dependencies:

```
$ gradle -q dependencies --configuration runtime


------------------------------------------------------------

Root project

------------------------------------------------------------


runtime - Runtime classpath for source set 'main'.
+--- org.slf4j:slf4j-api:1.7.7
\--- ch.qos.logback:logback-classic:1.1.2
     +--- ch.qos.logback:logback-core:1.1.2
     \--- org.slf4j:slf4j-api:1.7.6 -> 1.7.7


(*) - dependencies omitted (listed previously)
```

Customizing dependency resolution rules

For each dependency we define in our build file, there is a dependency resolution rule. This rule is executed when the dependency needs to be resolved. We can customize this rule in our build file, so we can change certain parts of the rule before the dependency is actually resolved. Gradle allows us to change the dependency group, name, and version with a customized resolution rule. This way, we can even completely replace dependencies with other dependencies or force a particular version.

Dependency resolution rule details are implemented in the `org.gradle.api.artifacts.DependencyResolveDetails` class. Inside the `resolutionStrategy` configuration block, we use the `eachDependency` method to customize a resolution rule. This method accepts a closure, and the closure argument is an instance of `DependencyResolveDetails`. We use the `useVersion` and `useTarget` methods of `DependencyResolveDetails` to change either the version or the complete group, name, and version for a requested dependency.

Let's change our previous example build file and define a customized resolution rule for the `org.slf4j:slf4j-api` dependency so that the version `1.7.7` is always used. In the next example build file, we will see how to achieve this:

```
apply plugin: 'java'

repositories.jcenter()

configurations {
  runtime {
    resolutionStrategy {
      failOnVersionConflict()

      // Customize dependency resolve rules.
      eachDependency { DependencyResolveDetails details ->
        def requestedModule = details.requested

        // Force version for
        // org.slf4j:slf4j-api dependency.
        if (requestedModule.group == 'org.slf4j'
          && requestedModule.name == 'slf4j-api') {

          // Force version 1.7.7.
          details.useVersion '1.7.7'
        }
      }
    }
  }
}

dependencies {
  compile 'org.slf4j:slf4j-api:1.7.7'

  runtime 'ch.qos.logback:logback-classic:1.1.2'
}
```

This mechanism is very powerful. Besides forcing a particular version, we can use the dependency resolution rules to replace a complete dependency with another. Let's suppose we have a dependency in our project and this dependency has a transitive dependency on the Log4j logging framework. We don't want this dependency, and instead want to use the log4j-over-slf4j bridge. This bridge contains alternative implementations for Log4j classes, so we can use an SLF4J API implementation. The log4j-over-slf4j bridge is defined by the `org.slf4j:log4j-over-slf4j:1.7.7` dependency. We use the `useTarget` method of the resolution rule details to set a new target. The method accepts both string notations and map notations for dependencies.

The following example build file contains the dependency resolution rule to replace a dependency on the `Log4j` to the `log4j-over-slf4j` bridge:

```
apply plugin: 'java'

repositories.jcenter()

configurations {
  runtime {
    resolutionStrategy {
      eachDependency { DependencyResolveDetails details ->
        def requestedModule = details.requested

        // Change resolve rule for log4j:log4j
        // (transitive) dependency.
        if (requestedModule.group == 'log4j'
          && requestedModule.name == 'log4j') {

          // Replace log4j:log4j:<version> with
          // org.slf4j:log4j-over-slf4j:1.7.7.
          details.useTarget group: 'org.slf4j',
                  name: 'log4j-over-slf4j',
                  version: '1.7.7'
          // Alternative syntax:
          // useTarget 'org.slf4j:log4j-over-slf4j:1.7.7'
        }
      }
    }
  }
}

dependencies {
```

```
    compile 'org.slf4j:slf4j-api:1.7.7'

    // In real life this is probably a transitive
    // dependency from a dependency we need in our project.
    // We put it here as an example to show we
    // can completely replace a dependency with
    // another.
    runtime 'log4j:log4j:1.2.17'

    runtime 'ch.qos.logback:logback-classic:1.1.2'
}
```

We can verify that the Log4j dependency is replaced with the `dependencies` task from the command line. This is shown in the following code:

```
$ gradle -q dependencies --configuration runtime


------------------------------------------------------------

Root project

------------------------------------------------------------


runtime - Runtime classpath for source set 'main'.
+--- org.slf4j:slf4j-api:1.7.7
+--- log4j:log4j:1.2.17 -> org.slf4j:log4j-over-slf4j:1.7.7
|     \--- org.slf4j:slf4j-api:1.7.7
\--- ch.qos.logback:logback-classic:1.1.2
     +--- ch.qos.logback:logback-core:1.1.2
     \--- org.slf4j:slf4j-api:1.7.6 -> 1.7.7


(*) - dependencies omitted (listed previously)
```

Notice the `log4j:log4j:1.2.17` → `org.slf4j:log4j-over-slf4j:1.7.7` line, which visually shows the replacement of the dependency with a new dependency.

Custom dependency resolution rules also allow us to define a custom version scheme. For example, in our organization, we can define that if the version of a dependency is set to the `fixed` value, the actual version is fetched from a central location on the corporate intranet. This way, all projects in the organization can share the same version for dependencies.

In the next example build file, we will implement a custom version scheme. If the version attribute is omitted or has the fixed value, then the version information is fetched from a predefined list of versions. The following code shows this:

```
apply plugin: 'java'

repositories.jcenter()

configurations {
  runtime {
    resolutionStrategy {
      eachDependency { DependencyResolveDetails details ->
        def requestedModule = details.requested

        // If version is not set or version
        // has value 'fixed' set
        // version based on external definition.
        if (!requestedModule.version
          || requestedModule.version == 'fixed') {
          def moduleVersion =
          findModuleVersion(requestedModule.name)
          details.useVersion moduleVersion
        }
      }
    }
  }
}

dependencies {
  // Version is not defined for this dependency,
  // is resolved via custom dependency resolve rule.
  compile 'org.slf4j:slf4j-api'

  // Version is set to 'fixed', so version can
  // be resolved via custom dependency resolve rule.
  runtime 'ch.qos.logback:logback-classic:fixed'
}

/**
 * Find version for given module name. In real life
 * this could be part of a company Gradle plugin
 * or intranet resource with version information.
 *
 * @param name Module descriptor name
```

```
 * @return Version for given module name
 */
def findModuleVersion(String name) {
   ['slf4j-api': '1.7.7', 'logback-classic': '1.1.2']
   .find { it.key == name}
   .value
}
```

It is interesting to see what the output of the `dependencies` task is when we run it from the command line:

```
$ gradle -q dependencies --configuration runtime


------------------------------------------------------------

Root project

------------------------------------------------------------


runtime - Runtime classpath for source set 'main'.
+--- org.slf4j:slf4j-api: -> 1.7.7
\--- ch.qos.logback:logback-classic: -> 1.1.2
     +--- ch.qos.logback:logback-core:1.1.2
     \--- org.slf4j:slf4j-api:1.7.6 -> 1.7.7


(*) - dependencies omitted (listed previously)
```

In the output, we clearly see how the `org.slf4j:slf4j-api` dependency without a version is now using the version `1.7.7`. The `fixed` version of the `ch.qos.logback:logback-classic` dependency is resolved to the version `1.1.2`.

Using client modules

Instead of relying on the module descriptor found in the repository for our external module dependency, we can define the metadata for the module in our build file as a client module. Remember from *Chapter 1*, *Defining Dependencies*, that with a client module, we define the module descriptor in our build file and still get the artifacts from the repository.

Let's use a client module in the following example build file. We redefine the transitive dependencies for the `logback-classic` dependency and use the version `1.7.7` for the `slf4j-api` dependency. The following code shows this:

```
apply plugin: 'java'

repositories.jcenter()

configurations {
  runtime {
    resolutionStrategy {
      failOnVersionConflict()
    }
  }
}

dependencies {
  compile 'org.slf4j:slf4j-api:1.7.7'

  // Use a client module to redefine the transitive
  // dependencies for the logback-classic.
  runtime module('ch.qos.logback:logback-classic:1.1.2') {
    dependency 'ch.qos.logback:logback-core:1.1.2'

    // Force the correct version of
    // the slf4j-api dependency/
    dependency 'org.slf4j:slf4j-api:1.7.7'
  }
}
```

We invoke the `dependencies` task from the command line to check whether the correct dependencies are used:

```
$ gradle -q dependencies --configuration runtime


------------------------------------------------------------
Root project
------------------------------------------------------------


runtime - Runtime classpath for source set 'main'.
+--- org.slf4j:slf4j-api:1.7.7
\--- ch.qos.logback:logback-classic:1.1.2
     +--- org.slf4j:slf4j-api:1.7.7
```

```
\--- ch.qos.logback:logback-core:1.1.2
```

```
(*) - dependencies omitted (listed previously)
```

We see in the output that the dependency on `org.slf4j:slf4j-api` is now `1.7.7` and we don't have version conflict anymore.

Using dynamic versions and changing modules

In *Chapter 1*, *Defining Dependencies*, we already learned about dynamic versions. For example, we can use a range of versions such as `[4.0.1.RELEASE,4.0.4.RELEASE[`. When the dependency is resolved by Gradle, the latest available static version in the range is selected.

A changing module is different than a dynamic version. A changing module references a dependency with the same version but with changing artifacts. For example, in a Maven repository, a changing module is the snapshot module indicated by `-SNAPSHOT` in the `version` attribute. Gradle can resolve a changing module dependency and get the latest artifact for the given version. However, the next time, a new artifact might be downloaded because the content has changed.

Gradle caches dynamic versions and changing modules for 24 hours. We will see how we can customize this behavior in our Gradle build file and from the command line. However, before we take a look at the options, we will first see how Gradle caching works.

Understanding the dependency cache

The dependency cache of Gradle tries to minimize the number of remote requests and downloads so that builds can be fast and reliable. The cache has two parts to perform proper dependency caching:

* First, it has a cache for dependency metadata (POM or Ivy descriptor files) for a dependency group, name, and version. Gradle keeps a separate cache for each repository. So, if the same dependency is found in multiple repositories, then the metadata information is cached in multiple dependency metadata caches.

* The dependency cache also has a single cache with downloaded artifacts for the dependencies. The multiple metadata caches share the same cache for downloaded artifacts. The artifacts are stored by the SHA1 hash code of their contents and not by metadata, such as group, name, or version.

The separation of a metadata cache based on the repository and the artifact cache provides enough flexibility to perform repeatable and reliable dependency resolution. If the dependency metadata cannot be resolved by Gradle, then the dependency resolution will stop, even if the local cache has a copy of the artifact that was downloaded from a different repository (not defined in our build). This repository independence isolates builds from each other and prevents problems with dependency artifacts.

Gradle first tries to determine the SHA1 checksum for an artifact file before downloading the artifact. If the checksum can be determined, the file will not be downloaded if it is already in the cache with the same checksum. Gradle also tries to reuse artifacts from the local Maven repository. If the checksum for an artifact in the local Maven repository matches the checksum for the artifact from the remote repository, then the artifact doesn't need to be downloaded and can be copied from the local Maven repository.

Because Gradle uses an SHA1 checksum for the artifact contents, different versions for the same artifact can be stored. For example, when an artifact is part of a changing module or the contents of the artifact have changed in the repository without a change in the version number.

Both the metadata cache and artifact cache are stored in the directory defined by the GRADLE_USER_HOME environment variable that is, by default, the .gradle/ caches directory in the user home directory. Gradle uses a sophisticated locking mechanism for the caches, so multiple projects can use the cache directories and files simultaneously. In the next example build file, we create the artifactsLocation task to print out where the downloaded artifacts are stored:

```
apply plugin: 'java'

repositories.jcenter()

dependencies {
  compile 'org.slf4j:slf4j-api:1.7.7'
  runtime 'ch.qos.logback:logback-classic:1.1.2'
}

task artifactsLocation {
  description 'Show location of artifact on disk'

  doFirst {
    configurations.runtime.each { println it }
  }
}
```

When we execute the `artifactsLocation` task, we see in the output that the files are stored in the `.gradle/caches` directory in the user home directory (`/Users/mrhaki`). We also see the SHA1 checksums with which the directory names are used. The following code shows this:

```
$ gradle -q artifactsLocation
/Users/mrhaki/.gradle/caches/modules-2/files-2.1/org.slf4j/slf4j-api/1.7.
7/2b8019b6249bb05d81d3a3094e468753e2b21311/slf4j-api-1.7.7.jar

/Users/mrhaki/.gradle/caches/modules-2/files-2.1/ch.qos.logback/logback-
classic/1.1.2/b316e9737eea25e9ddd6d88eaeee76878045c6b2/logback-classic-
1.1.2.jar

/Users/mrhaki/.gradle/caches/modules-2/files-2.1/ch.qos.logback/logback-
core/1.1.2/2d23694879c2c12f125dac5076bdfd5d771cc4cb/logback-core-1.1.2.
jar
```

Command-line options for caching

We can use the `--offline` command-line option to skip any network requests. So, with this option, Gradle never tries to access remote repositories and all information is fetched from the Gradle dependency caches. If the information in the caches is not sufficient for a build, then the build fails.

With the `--refresh-dependencies` option, we can refresh the metadata caches. If, for some reason, we expect the metadata to be no longer correct, we can use this option. Gradle will then refresh all information in the metadata caches for each repository. Artifacts are only downloaded when the SHA1 checksum is different than the checksum for artifacts in the artifacts cache.

Changing cache expiration

A dependency with a static version can be easily cached. The contents of the artifact has a checksum, and this can be used to either use the cache or download the artifact (and place it in the artifact cache). A dependency with a dynamic version or changing module can have a changing artifact, so we need to be able to customize the cache settings. We can change the expiration time for cached dependencies with a dynamic version and changing modules. The default expiration time is 24 hours. After the expiration time, Gradle will invalidate the cache and determine whether an artifact needs to be downloaded again.

We change the expiration time for dependencies with a dynamic version using the `cacheDynamicVersionsFor` method of the `resolutionStrategy` configuration closure. The method accepts a number and time unit to set the value for the cache expiration. The time unit can be either of the `java.util.concurrent.TimeUnit` type or a string that is converted to `TimeUnit`.

To change modules, we use the `cacheChangingModulesFor` method to change the expiration time. This method also accepts a number and time unit just as the `cacheDynamicVersionsFor` method does.

In the next example build file, we change the cache expiration for both dynamic versions and changing modules for `runtime` configurations. We can also set it for all configurations with the `all` method and configuration block. The following code shows this:

```
// Import needed for cache methods time unit.
import java.util.concurrent.TimeUnit

apply plugin: 'java'

repositories.jcenter()

configurations {
  runtime {
    resolutionStrategy {
        // Change expiration time for caching
        // dynamic version to 30 minutes.
        cacheDynamicVersionsFor 30, 'minutes'

        // Alternative syntax is using TimeUnit:
        // cacheDynamicVersionsFor 1, TimeUnit.HOURS

        // Change expiration time for cached
        // changing modules to 5 minutes using
        // java.util.concurrent.TimeUnit.
        cacheChangingModulesFor 5, TimeUnit.MINUTES

        // Or we could use string notation.
        // cacheChangingModulesFor 1, 'minutes'
    }
  }

  // Alternatively we could apply
  // this to all configurations:
  // all {
```

```
//        resolutionStrategy {
//            cacheDynamicVersionsFor 4, 'hours'
//            cacheChangingModulesFor 10, 'minutes'
//        }
// }
}

dependencies {
  compile 'org.slf4j:slf4j-api:1.7.7'

  runtime 'ch.qos.logback:logback-classic:1.1.2'
}
```

Gradle knows about artifacts that are stored in a Maven repository, and that if the version attribute ends with -SNAPSHOT, the module is a changing module. We can also define in our build script whether a dependency is a changing module, for example, if this cannot be derived from the version attribute. We must set the changing property to the value true in the configuration closure for a dependency.

In the following example build file, we have the com.vehicles:cars dependency, which is a changing module, but we use the static version 1.0:

```
apply plugin: 'java'

repositories {
  maven {
    url 'http://ourcompany.com/maven'
  }
}

dependencies {
  compile('com.vehicles:cars:1.0') {
    // Instruct Gradle this a changing
    // module, although it cannot
    // be derived from the version attribute.
    changing = true
  }

  // Other syntax using the map notation:
  // compile group: 'com.vehicles', name: 'cars',
  //          version: '1.0', changing: true
}
```

Summary

In this chapter, you learned how Gradle resolves dependencies and how to customize this. You saw how to reconfigure your build scripts to handle transitive dependencies and how to resolve version conflicts between dependencies in your builds. Gradle offers some fine-grained control on how we define dependencies and allows very explicit dependency definitions.

For transitive dependencies, we have several ways to redefine which dependencies need to be used by either disabling or excluding transitive dependencies.

When a version conflict arises between dependencies in our build, we can either rely on the default strategy of using the newest version or implement a custom strategy. Gradle has several ways to customize dependency resolution rules by redefining the resolution strategy. For example, we can override the version attribute for a dependency or even totally replace it with a compatible but different dependency.

Finally, you saw how the dependency cache of Gradle works. It is designed to reduce network requests and provide reliable and repeatable builds that have dependencies. You learned how you can customize the expiration time for dependency modules that are changing or are defined with dynamic versions.

Up until now, we saw how to include dependencies in our projects, but in the next chapter, we will see how we can publish artifacts that we created as dependencies for other projects.

4
Publishing Artifacts

In the previous chapters, we learned how to define and use dependencies in our projects. However, the code we write in our projects can also be a dependency for another project. In order for another project to use our code as a dependency, we should publish our code as a dependency artifact so that it can be used by other projects.

In this chapter, you will learn how you can define artifacts in your project. These artifacts need to be published for others to use them. We first publish them using a filesystem, so the artifacts can be used from the same computer or even if we use a network share on an intranet. In later chapters, we will see how to publish our artifacts to a Maven repository, an Ivy repository, and Bintray.

Defining artifact configurations

A Gradle project can contain artifacts we want to publish. An artifact can be a ZIP or JAR archive file or any other file. We can define one or more artifacts in one project. Thus, we don't have to create two different projects if we want to have two different artifacts from the same source tree.

In Gradle, we group artifacts using configurations. We used configurations to define dependencies for our project, but now we will use the configurations to group our artifacts that can be dependencies for others. So a configuration can contain both dependencies and artifacts. If we apply the Java plugin to our project, we get a configuration named `archives`, that contains the default JAR artifact for the project.

In the following example Gradle build file, we use the Java plugin. We add a task to display the filename of the artifact that belongs to the `archives` configuration. The following code shows this:

```
apply plugin: 'java'

// Set the archivesBaseName property,
// to change the name of the
// default project artifact.
archivesBaseName = 'java_lib'

task artifactsInfo << {
  // Find archives configuration
  // and display file name(s)
  // for artifacts belonging
  // to the configuration.
  configurations
    .findByName('archives')
    .allArtifacts
    .each { artifact ->
      println artifact.file.name
    }
}
```

When we run the `artifactsInfo` task from the command line, we see the `java_lib.jar` filename in the output. The following code shows this:

```
$ gradle artifactsInfo
:artifactsInfo
java_lib.jar

BUILD SUCCESSFUL

Total time: 1.088 secs
```

For each configuration in our project, Gradle adds two tasks to the project: `build<ConfigurationName>` and `upload<ConfigurationName>`. The `build<ConfigurationName>` task creates the artifacts for the given configuration name. The `upload<ConfigurationName>` task creates and uploads the artifacts for the given configuration name. The `upload<ConfigurationName>` task needs extra configuration to know where to upload the artifacts. We will see later in this chapter how to configure the task.

In our example project, we have the `buildArchives` and `uploadArchives` tasks.
Let's run the `buildArchives` task for our example project and see which tasks
are executed:

```
$ gradle buildArchives
:compileJava
:processResources
:classes
:jar
:buildArchives

BUILD SUCCESSFUL

Total time: 1.209 secs
$ ls build/libs
java_lib.jar
```

Here, we can see that first everything is prepared in our Java project to create the
JAR artifact. The JAR artifact is then added to the `artifacts` configuration. The
`java_lib.jar` JAR file that is created can be found in the `build/libs` directory.

If we set the `version` property for our project, then it will be used in the name of our
created artifact. In the next example build file, we will set the `version` property and
look at the name that is created for the artifact:

```
apply plugin: 'java'

archivesBaseName = 'java_lib'

// Set project version,
// which is then used in the
// artifact name.
version = '2.3'

task artifactsInfo << {
configurations
    .findByName('archives')
    .allArtifacts
    .each { artifact ->
      println artifact.file.name
    }
}
```

Let's run the `artifactsInfo` task to see the name of our artifact:

```
$ gradle artifactsInfo
:artifactsInfo
java_lib-2.3.jar

BUILD SUCCESSFUL

Total time: 2.831 secs
```

Defining artifacts

In the previous section, you learned that the Java plugin adds an `archives` configuration that is used to group artifacts from the project. Just as we created configurations for dependencies in our project, we can also create our own configurations for its artifacts. To assign an archive or file to this configuration, we must use the `artifacts` configuration block in our build script. Inside the configuration closure, we use the name of the configuration followed by the artifact. We can also further customize the artifact definition inside the `artifacts` block.

We can define artifacts with the following three types:

Type	Description
AbstractArchiveTask	The information for the artifact is extracted from the archive task. The artifact is an instance of `PublishArtifact` in the `org.gradle.api.artifacts` package.
File	The information for the artifact is extracted from the filename. The artifact is an instance of `ConfigurablePublishArtifact` that extends `PublishArtifact`.
Map	This is another way to define a file artifact. The map must contain a `file` key, and other properties are used to further configure the artifact.

Using the archive task

In the next example build file, we will use an archive task to define the artifacts for the project. It is important to remember to apply the Gradle base plugin to the project because the base plugin adds the task rules for build<ConfigurationName> and upload<ConfigurationName>. The following code shows this:

```
// The base plugin adds the
// build<ConfigurationName> and
// upload<ConfigurationName> tasks
// to our project.
apply plugin: 'base'

// Add archive task that will
// create a ZIP file with some
// contents we want to be published.
task manual(type: Zip) {
  baseName = 'manual'

  from 'src/manual'
}

// Create a new artifacts configuration
// with the name manualDistribution.
configurations {
  manualDistribution
}

// Use the manual archive task
// to define the artifact for the
// manualDistribution configuration.
// Syntax:
// configurationName archiveTask
artifacts {
  manualDistribution manual
}
```

When we use an archive task to define the artifact for a configuration, Gradle also adds a task dependency for the artifact. This means that, if we invoke the `buildManualDistribution` task, Gradle also invokes the `manual` task that generates the archive for the artifact configuration. We see this when we execute the task from the command line. The following command shows this:

```
$ gradle buildManualDistribution
:manual
:buildManualDistribution


BUILD SUCCESSFUL


Total time: 1.368 secs
```

Using artifact files

Besides archive tasks, we can use a file as an artifact. Gradle will use the properties of the file to define the artifact name, type, and extension. In the following example build file, we use a file as an artifact:

```
apply plugin: 'base'

configurations {
  readmeDistribution
}

artifacts {
  // Use a file as artifact.
  // Name and extension are extracted
  // from the actual file.
  readmeDistribution file('src/files/README.txt')
}
```

We can add an extra configuration closure when we use the file artifact notation. In the closure, we can set the name, type, extension, and classifier attributes. The following code shows this:

```
apply plugin: 'base'

configurations {
  readmeDistribution
}

artifacts {
```

```
// Define file artifact, but we also
// customize the file artifact
// name, extension and classifier.
readmeDistribution file('src/files/README.txt'), {
  name 'PLEASE_READ_THIS'
  extension ''
  classifier 'docs'
}
}
```

One interesting method we can use in the file artifact configuration closure is the `builtBy` method. This method accepts one or more task names that are responsible for building the artifact. If we use this method, Gradle can determine the tasks that need to be executed when we run the `build<ConfigurationName>` or `upload<ConfigurationName>` task.

We will use the `builtBy` method in the next example build file:

```
apply plugin: 'base'

configurations {
  readmeDistribution
}

// New task that copies
// a file to the build directory.
task docFiles(type:Copy) {
  from 'src/files'
  into "${buildDir}/docs"
  include 'README.txt'
}

artifacts {
  // Define file artifact.
  readmeDistribution(file("${buildDir}/docs/README.txt")) {
    // Define which task is responsible
    // for creating the file, so a
    // task dependency is added for
    // the buildReadmeDistribution and
    // uploadReadmeDistribution tasks.
    builtBy docFiles
  }
}
```

To ensure that the `docFiles` task is added as a task dependency, we run the `buildReadmeDistribution` from the command line. The following command shows this:

```
$ gradle buildReadmeDistribution
:docFiles
:buildReadmeDistribution

BUILD SUCCESSFUL

Total time: 0.864 secs
```

Finally, we can use a map notation when we define a file artifact. We use the `file` attribute to define the file. We can also use the `name`, `extension`, `type`, `classifier`, and `builtBy` keys for the definition. In the following example build file, we use the map notation:

```
apply plugin: 'base'

configurations {
  readmeDistribution
}

task docFiles(type:Copy) {
  from 'src/files'
  into "${buildDir}/docs"
  include 'README.txt'
}

artifacts {
  // Define file artifact.
  readmeDistribution(
    file: "${buildDir}/docs/README.txt",
    name: 'DO_READ',
    extension: 'me',
    type: 'text',
    classifier: 'docs'
    builtBy: docFiles
  )
}
```

Creating artifacts

We saw how to define artifacts, but we also need to create artifacts in our build files. We can either use an archive task to create the artifact or a file can be an artifact. Most of the time, when we use Gradle in a Java project, we build an archive with compiled classes and resources. Actually, the Java plugin adds a `jar` task to our project that will just do that. The JAR file created is then added to the `archives` configuration.

In the next example build file, we will use the Java plugin and simply rely on the default artifact configuration and tasks. The following code shows this:

```
apply plugin: 'java'

// Define project properties.
group = 'com.mrhaki.sample'
version = '2.1'
archivesBaseName = 'sample'

// Extra task to check the artifacts.
task artifactsInfo << {
  configurations
    .findByName('archives')
    .allArtifacts
    .each { artifact ->
      println artifact.file.name
    }
}
```

We can now run the `buildArchives` task and check the artifacts with the `artifactsInfo` task from the command line:

```
$ gradle buildArchives artifactsInfo
:compileJava
:processResources
:classes
:jar
:buildArchives
:artifactsInfo
sample-2.1.jar

BUILD SUCCESSFUL

Total time: 7.643 secs
$
```

In this case, we have a single artifact; however, in the same project we can have more than one artifact when we use Gradle. For example, we might want to have our source packaged into a JAR file and our generated documentation as well. Both JAR files should be part of the `archives` configuration so that, when we execute the `buildArchives` task, all the tasks necessary to create these JAR files are executed.

We extend our previous example build file, add the code to create two extra JAR files, and add them to the `archives` artifact configuration. The following code shows this:

```
apply plugin: 'java'

// Define project properties.
group = 'com.mrhaki.sample'
version = '2.1'
archivesBaseName = 'sample'

// Create a JAR file with the
// Java source files.
task sourcesJar(type: Jar) {
  classifier = 'sources'

  from sourceSets.main.allJava
}

// Create a JAR file with the output
// of the javadoc task.
task javadocJar(type: Jar) {
  classifier = 'javadoc'

  from javadoc
}

artifacts {
  // Add the new archive tasks
  // to the artifacts configuration.
  archives sourcesJar, javadocJar
}

// Extra task to check the artifacts.
task artifactsInfo << {
  configurations
    .findByName('archives')
    .allArtifacts
```

```
    .each { artifact ->
      println artifact.file.name
    }
  }
}
```

We will now execute the `buildArchives` and `artifactsInfo` tasks. We see in the
output that our two new tasks, `sourcesJar` and `javadocJar`, are executed. And
the generated artifact files are `sample-2.1.jar`, `sample-2.1-sources.jar`, and
`sample-2.1-javadoc.jar`. The following command shows this:

```
$ gradle buildArchives artifactsInfo
:compileJava
:processResources
:classes
:jar
:javadoc
:javadocJar
:sourcesJar
:buildArchives
:artifactsInfo
sample-2.1.jar
sample-2.1-sources.jar
sample-2.1-javadoc.jar

BUILD SUCCESSFUL

Total time: 2.945 secs
$
```

In the preceding example, we have a Java project and, from the same source set, we
want to create two different archive files. The source set contains a few API classes
and implementation classes. We want to have a JAR file with the API classes and a
JAR file, along with the implementation classes. The following code shows this:

```
apply plugin: 'java'

// Define project properties.
group = 'com.mrhaki.sample'
version = '2.1'
```

```
    archivesBaseName = 'sample'

    // We create a new source set
    // api, which contains the
    // Java sources. This means
    // Gradle will search for the
    // directory src/api/java.
    sourceSets {
      api
    }

    task apiJar(type: Jar) {
      appendix = 'api'

      // We use the output of the
      // compilation of the api
      // source set, to be the
      // contents of this JAR file.
      from sourceSets.api.output
    }

    artifacts {
      // Assign apiJar archive task to the
      // archives configuration.
      archives apiJar
    }

    // Extra task to check the artifacts.
    task artifactsInfo << {
      configurations
        .findByName('archives')
        .allArtifacts
        .each { artifact ->
          println artifact.file.name
        }
    }
```

We will now run the `buildArchives` task and see that all the tasks necessary to create the JAR file with the classes from the `api` source set are executed:

```
$ gradle buildArchives artifactsInfo
:compileApiJava
:processApiResources
:apiClasses
```

```
:apiJar

:compileJava

:processResources

:classes

:jar

:buildArchives

:artifactsInfo

sample-2.1.jar

sample-api-2.1.jar


BUILD SUCCESSFUL


Total time: 2.095 secs
$
```

Publishing artifacts to the local directory

We now know how to create one or more artifacts and how to use artifact configurations to group them. In this section, we will see how we can copy our artifacts to a local directory or network share. Remember that, for each artifact's configuration, Gradle adds a `build<ConfigurationName>` task and an `upload<ConfigurationName>` task. Now it is time to learn more about the `upload<ConfigurationName>` task so that we can copy our artifacts. In the following chapters we will also learn how to deploy to a Maven repository, an Ivy repository, and to Bintray.

For each `upload<ConfigurationName>` task, we must configure a repository definition. The repository definition is basically the destination of our artifacts when we upload or publish them. In this section, we use a local directory, so we define a repository using the `flatDir` method. We specify a name and the directory so that Gradle knows where the output of the `upload<ConfigurationName>` task needs to go. In Gradle projects where we have applied the Java plugin, we already have the `archives` artifact configuration and the `uploadArchives` task. We must configure the `uploadArchives` task and define the repository that needs to be used. In the next example build file, we will use the `lib-repo` local directory as the repository directory:

```
apply plugin: 'java'

// Define project properties.
group = 'com.mrhaki.sample'
version = '2.1'
```

```
    archivesBaseName = 'sample'

    // Configure the uploadArchives task.
    uploadArchives {
      // Define a local directory as the
      // upload repository. The artifacts
      // must be 'published' in this
      // directory.
      repositories {
        flatDir(
          name: 'upload-repository',
          dirs: "${projectDir}/lib-repo")
      }
    }
```

Let's see the output when we execute the uploadArchives task and check the files in the lib-repo directory:

```
$ gradle uploadArchives
:compileJava UP-TO-DATE
:processResources UP-TO-DATE
:classes UP-TO-DATE
:jar UP-TO-DATE
:uploadArchives

BUILD SUCCESSFUL

Total time: 3.424 secs
$ ls -1 lib-repo
ivy-2.1.xml
ivy-2.1.xml.sha1
sample-2.1.jar
sample-2.1.jar.sha1
$
```

In our `lib-repo` directory, for our artifact, we have an Ivy descriptor file named `ivy-2.1.xml` and, for this descriptor file, a checksum file named `ivy-2.1.xml.sha1`. Also, we see our `sample-2.1.jar` artifact and the `sample-2.1.jar.sha1` checksum file for our artifact. The Ivy descriptor file contains basic information about our artifact. This is shown by the following code:

```
<?xml version="1.0" encoding="UTF-8"?>
<ivy-module version="2.0" xmlns:m="http://ant.apache.org/ivy/maven">
  <info organisation="com.mrhaki.sample" module="java"
revision="2.1" status="integration" publication="20141126060840">
    <description/>
  </info>
  <configurations>
    <conf name="archives" visibility="public"
description="Configuration for archive artifacts."/>
    <conf name="compile" visibility="private" description="Compile
classpath for source set 'main'."/>
    <conf name="default" visibility="public"
description="Configuration for default artifacts."
extends="runtime"/>
    <conf name="runtime" visibility="private" description="Runtime
classpath for source set 'main'." extends="compile"/>
    <conf name="testCompile" visibility="private"
description="Compile classpath for source set 'test'."
extends="compile"/>
    <conf name="testRuntime" visibility="private"
description="Runtime classpath for source set 'test'."
extends="runtime,testCompile"/>
  </configurations>
  <publications>
    <artifact name="sample" type="jar" ext="jar"
conf="archives,runtime"/>
  </publications>
</ivy-module>
```

We have configured the repository inside the `uploadArchives` task configuration. However, we can also refer to an existing repository definition that was configured in our project using the `repositories` configuration block. This is a good practice because we only have to define the repository once and can reuse it in multiple tasks in our build files. Let's rewrite our previous example build file, define the repository in a `repositories` configuration block, and refer to it from the `uploadArchives` task. The following code shows this:

```
apply plugin: 'java'

// Define project properties.
group = 'com.mrhaki.sample'
version = '2.1'
archivesBaseName = 'sample'

// Define upload repository.
repositories {
  flatDir(
    name: 'upload-repository',
    dirs: "${projectDir}/repo")
}


// Configure the uploadArchives task.
uploadArchives {
  // Refer to repository with the
  // name 'upload-repository' as the
  // repository for uploading artifacts.
  repositories.add(
    project.repositories.'upload-repository')
}
```

Excluding the descriptor file

By default, an Ivy descriptor file is added to the upload location. If we don't want it, we can set the `uploadDescriptor` property for the `Upload` task.

In the following example build file, we set the `uploadDescriptor` property to `false` in the `uploadArchives` task:

```
apply plugin: 'java'

// Define project properties.
group = 'com.mrhaki.sample'
```

```
version = '2.1'
archivesBaseName = 'sample'

// Define upload repository.
repositories {
  flatDir(
    name: 'upload-repository',
    dirs: "${projectDir}/lib-repo")
}

uploadArchives {
  // Exclude the descriptor file.
  uploadDescriptor = false

  repositories.add(
    project.repositories.'upload-repository')
}
```

When we execute the task and look at the files in the `lib-repo` directory, we see that the descriptor file is not added. The following code shows this:

```
$ gradle uploadArchives
:compileJava
:processResources
:classes
:jar
:uploadArchives

BUILD SUCCESSFUL

Total time: 1.463 secs
$ ls -1 lib-repo
sample-2.1.jar
sample-2.1.jar.sha1
$
```

Signing artifacts

We can digitally sign artifacts in Gradle with the signing plugin. The plugin supports generating **Pretty Good Privacy** (**PGP**) signatures. This signature format is also required for publication to Maven Central Repository. To create a PGP signature, we must install a few PGP tools on our computer. Installation of the tools is different for each operating system. On Unix-like systems, the software is probably available via a package manager. With the PGP software, we need to create a key pair that we can use to sign artifacts.

To sign artifacts, we must apply the signing plugin to our project. Then we must configure the plugin using a `signing` configuration block. We need to at least add information about our PGP key pair. We need the hexadecimal representation of the public key, the path to the secret key ring file with our private key, and the passphrase used to protect the private key. We assign this information to the `keyId`, `secretKeyRingFile`, and `password` properties of the signing plugin configuration. These values shouldn't be part of the Gradle build file because they are secret, so it is better to store them in a `gradle.properties` file and apply secure file permissions to the file. Also, we do not add this file to our version control system.

In the following example `gradle.properties` file, we set the properties. The values are sample values and are different for each user:

```
signing.keyId = 8B00165A
signing.secretKeyRingFile = /Users/current/.gnupg/secring.gpg
signing.password = secret
```

Using configurations to sign

We are ready to sign our artifacts. We need to configure which artifacts we want to be signed using the `signing` configuration block. We must specify the name of the artifact configuration that contains the artifacts to be signed.

When we apply the Java plugin to our project, we get the `archives` artifact configuration. We want to sign the artifacts assigned to this configuration. In the next example build file, we apply both the Java and signing plugins. In the `signing` configuration block, we define that we want to sign the artifacts belonging to the `archives` configuration:

```
apply plugin: 'java'
apply plugin: 'signing'

group = 'com.mrhaki.sample'
version = '2.1'
```

```
archivesBaseName = 'sample'

// Configure signing plugin.
signing {
  // Define that we want to
  // sign the artifacts belonging
  // to the archives configuration.
  sign configurations.archives
}

uploadArchives {
  repositories {
    flatDir(
      name: 'local-repo',
      dirs: "${projectDir}/repo")
  }
}
```

The signing plugin also adds a new task rule to our project—
`sign<ConfigurationName>`. The name of the configuration is what we define in
the `signing` configuration block. We defined the `archives` configuration so, in our
project, we can now execute the `signArchives` task. The task is also added as a task
dependency to the assemble task; thus, every time we invoke the `assemble` task,
Gradle makes sure the `signArchives` task is invoked as well.

Here, we run the `uploadArchives` task to see which files are put in the
repository directory:

$ gradle uploadArchives

:compileJava

:processResources

:classes

:jar

:signArchives

:uploadArchives

BUILD SUCCESSFUL

Total time: 4.305 secs

$ ls -1 repo

ivy-2.1.xml

ivy-2.1.xml.sha1

```
sample-2.1.asc
sample-2.1.asc.sha1
sample-2.1.jar
sample-2.1.jar.sha1
$
```

We notice that a signature file, `sample-2.1.asc`, is created together with the `sample-2.1.asc.sha1` checksum file for the signature file.

Using archive tasks to sign

To sign an artifact that is not part of an artifact configuration, we must configure the signing plugin differently. In the `signing` configuration block, we assigned a configuration in the previous section, but we can also use an archive task. The output of this archive task will be signed when we invoke the `sign<TaskName>` task rule.

In the next example build file, we will create a ZIP file with the `manualZip` task. We will configure the signing plugin for the `manualZip` task so that this ZIP file is signed:

```
apply plugin: 'signing'

version = '1.0'

// New archive task to create
// a ZIP file from some files.
task manualZip(type: Zip) {
  archivesBaseName = 'manual'
  from 'src/docroot'
}

// Configure signing plugin to
// sign the output of the
// manualZip task.
signing {
  sign manualZip
}

// Create new configuration for
// ZIP and signed ZIP artifacts.
configurations {
```

```
    manualDistribution
  }

  // Set artifacts to manualDistribution
  // configuration.
  artifacts {
    manualDistribution(
      manualZip,
      signManualZip.singleSignature.file)
  }

  // Configure upload task for
  // manualDistribution configuration.
  uploadManualDistribution {
    repositories {
      flatDir {
        dirs "${projectDir}/repo"
      }
    }
  }
  // Add task dependency so signing of
  // ZIP file is done before upload.
  uploadManualDistribution.dependsOn signManualZip
```

All `sign<TaskName>` tasks automatically have a task dependency on the archive task identifier by `<TaskName>`. So, we can now simply invoke the `uploadManualDistribution` task, and the ZIP file is created, signed, and uploaded to the `repo` directory. The following code shows this:

```
$ gradle uploadManualDistribution
:manualZip
:signManualZip
:uploadManualDistribution

BUILD SUCCESSFUL

Total time: 1.695 secs
$ ls -1 repo
ivy-1.0.xml
ivy-1.0.xml.sha1
```

```
manual-1.0.zip
manual-1.0.zip-1.0.asc
manual-1.0.zip-1.0.asc.sha1
manual-1.0.zip.sha1
$
```

Summary

In the previous chapters, you learned how to use external dependencies. In this chapter, you learned how you can define artifact configurations to assign your own artifacts. These artifacts can be dependencies for other developers on other projects and applications.

You also learned how to create a default artifact when you use the Java plugin. Next, we saw how to create more than one artifact from the same project.

You then learned how to configure an Upload task, so you can upload your artifacts to a local directory. This directory could also be a network share accessible to other development teams.

Finally, you learned how you can sign your artifacts using the signing plugin. This could be useful when you want to provide some extra confidence to people using the artifacts.

In the next chapters, you will see how you can upload your artifacts to a Maven repository, an Ivy repository, and Bintray.

5
Publishing to a
Maven Repository

In the previous chapter, you learned how to use the `Upload` task to publish
your project artifacts. In this chapter, you will learn more about the new and
still-developing feature of publishing your artifacts to a Maven repository.

You will learn about the new publishing mechanism in Gradle. This feature is
currently still under development, and that means the implementation might
change in the future. But for now, this way of publishing artifacts will be the default.

Defining publication

We must add the `maven-publish` plugin to our project to add the new publication
feature of Gradle. The plugin allows us to define and deploy our project artifacts in
the Maven format. This means our deployed project can be used by other developers
and projects that support the Maven format. For example, other projects could use
Gradle or Maven and define a dependency to our published artifacts.

The `maven-publish` plugin is based on a general `publishing` plugin. The
`publishing` plugin adds a new `publishing` extension to our project. We can use
a `publications` configuration block in our build script to configure the artifacts
we want to publish and the repositories we want to deploy to. The `publications`
extension has the `PublishingExtension` type in the `org.gradle.api.publish`
package. The plugin also adds the general life cycle `publish` task to the project.
Other tasks can be added as task dependencies to this task; thus, with a single
`publish` task, all the publications in the project can be published.

The `maven-publish` plugins also add extra task rules to the project. There is a task to generate a Maven POM file for each publication in the project. The plugins also add a new task rule to publish each publication to the local Maven repository. Finally, a task rule is added based on a combination of the publication and the repository, to publish a publication to the specified repository.

Let's create an example build file and apply the `maven-publish` plugin to see the new task:

```
apply plugin: 'maven-publish'
apply plugin: 'java'
```

Now, we will invoke the `tasks` task from the command line:

```
$ gradle tasks

...

Publishing tasks
----------------

publish - Publishes all publications produced by this project.
publishToMavenLocal - Publishes all Maven publications produced by
this project to the local Maven cache.

...

BUILD SUCCESSFUL


Total time: 4.647 secs
```

We can see the `publish` and `publishToMavenLocal` tasks in the output. The dynamic task rules for publishing single publications to repositories are not shown.

To configure our publications, we must first add a `publishing` configuration block. Inside the block, we define the `publications` configuration block. In this block, we define a publication. A publication defines what needs to be published. The `maven-publish` plugin expects a publication to have the `MavenPublication` type found in the `org.gradle.api.publish.maven` package. Besides the artifacts that need to be published, we can also define details for the generated POM file.

Defining publication artifacts

Any publication we define must have a unique name in our project. We can add multiple publications with their own names inside a `publications` configuration block. To add an artifact, we can use the `artifact` method in the publication definition. We can also use the `artifacts` property to directly set all artifacts.

We can define artifacts with the `artifact` method in the following ways:

Type	Description
AbstractArchiveTask	The information for the artifact is extracted from the archive task. The artifact is an instance of `PublishArtifact` in the `org.gradle.api.artifacts` package.
File	The information for the artifact is extracted from the filename.
Map	This is another way to define artifacts. The map must contain a `source` key referencing a file or archive task. The other properties we can use to further configure the artifact are `classifier` and `extension`.

Using archive task artifacts

In the following example build file, we define a new publication with the name `publishJar`, and we define the output of the `jar` archive task as an artifact:

```
apply plugin: 'maven-publish'
apply plugin: 'java'

// Configuration block for publishing
// artifacts from the project.
publishing {

  // Define publications with what
  // needs to be published.
  publications {

    // Name of this publication
    // is publishJar.
    publishJar(MavenPublication) {

      // Use output of jar task
      // as the artifact for
      // the publication.
      artifact jar

      // Alternatively we can use
      // a Map notation:
      // artifact source: jar
    }

  }
}
```

Next, we will run the `tasks` task and, in the output, we will be able to see newly generated tasks for publishing this publication:

```
$ gradle tasks

...

Publishing tasks
----------------

generatePomFileForPublishJarPublication - Generates the Maven POM file
for publication 'publishJar'.

publish - Publishes all publications produced by this project.

publishPublishJarPublicationToMavenLocal - Publishes Maven publication
'publishJar' to the local Maven repository.

publishToMavenLocal - Publishes all Maven publications produced by this
project to the local Maven cache.

...

BUILD SUCCESSFUL


Total time: 4.215 secs
```

Notice the two extra tasks, `generatePomFileForPublishJarPublication` and `publishPublishJarPublicationToMavenLocal`. The name of the publication, `publishJar`, is used for the two tasks. Gradle uses the `generatePomFileFor<publicationName>Publication` pattern for a task to generate a POM for a publication. The task pattern to publish a publication to the local Maven repository is `publish<publicationName>PublicationToMavenLocal`. Later in this chapter, we will see how we can add other repositories. We cannot yet invoke the tasks because we also need to set the `group` and `version` project properties, but we will cover this in the section about generating a POM file. We can now focus on defining the artifacts for a publication in this section.

We are not restricted to one artifact for a publication; we can add more by invoking the `artifact` method multiple times. Or, we can use the `artifacts` property to assign multiple artifacts. It is important that each artifact should have unique `classifier` and `extension` property values for a single publication. Gradle will check this before we can invoke any tasks, so we immediately get an error message when the artifacts don't have a unique combination of `classifier` and `extensions` property values.

In the following example build file, we add two extra artifacts to our publication with the `artifact` method:

```
apply plugin: 'maven-publish'
apply plugin: 'java'

task sourcesJar(type: Jar) {
  from sourceSets.main.allJava
  classifier = 'sources'
}

task javadocJar(type: Jar) {
  from javadoc
}

publishing {

  publications {

    publishJar(MavenPublication) {

      artifact jar

      artifact sourcesJar

      artifact javadocJar {
        // Each artifact must have
        // a unique classifier.
        // We can set the classifier
        // via the task as in sourcesJar
        // or here in the artifact configuration.
        classifier = 'javadoc'
      }

      // Or with a Map notation we
      // can write:
      // artifact source: javadocJar, classifier: 'javadoc'

    }

  }
}
```

Instead of using the `artifact` method, we can also use the `artifacts` property and assign multiple artifacts. Each of the artifacts we assign must have a unique combination of `classifier` and `extension` property values. In the next example build file, we will use the same artifacts as in the previous example but, this time, we will assign them to the `artifacts` property:

```
apply plugin: 'maven-publish'
apply plugin: 'java'

task sourcesJar(type: Jar) {
  from sourceSets.main.allJava
  classifier = 'sources'
}

task javadocJar(type: Jar) {
  from javadoc
  classifier = 'javadoc'
}

publishing {

  publications {

    publishJar(MavenPublication) {

      // Use artifacts property to
      // define the artifacts.
      // The classifier for each of
      // these artifacts must be
      // unique.
      artifacts = [
        jar,
        sourcesJar,
        javaDocJar]

    }

  }
}
```

Using file artifacts

Instead of an archive task, we can also use a file as an artifact. Gradle tries to extract the `extension` and `classifier` properties from the filename. We can also configure these properties ourselves when we add the file as a publication artifact.

In the following example build file, we use the `src/files/README` and `src/files/COPYRIGHT` files as publication artifacts:

```
apply plugin: 'maven-publish'

publishing {
  publications {
    documentation(MavenPublication) {

      // Use file name as a publication artifact.
      artifact 'src/files/README'

      artifact('src/files/COPYRIGHT') {
        // Each file artifact must have a
        // unique classifier and extension.
        classifier = 'metaInformation'
      }

      // Alternative syntax is with
      // the Map notation:
      // artifact source: 'src/files/README'
      // artifact source: 'src/files/COPYRIGHT',
      //            extension: 'metaInformation'

    }
  }
}
```

Using software components

Besides the `artifact` method and the `artifacts` property, we can also use the `from` method inside a `publications` configuration block. We specify `SoftwareComponent` for Gradle as an argument to the `from` method. The `java` plugin adds `SoftwareComponent` with the name `java`, and it includes the `jar` artifact and all runtime dependencies. The `war` plugin adds the `war` artifact as `SoftwareComponent`. `SoftwareComponent` is a part of the Gradle build model that defines a piece of code that depends on other code or is a dependency for other code.

In the next example build file, we will apply the `war` plugin to our project, which will implicitly add the `java` plugin. We also define two publications, each using `SoftwareComponent` from both plugins. The following code shows this:

```
apply plugin: 'maven-publish'
apply plugin: 'war'


publishing {

  publications {

    // First publication with
    // the name javaJar, contains
    // the artifact created by the
    // jar task.
    javaJar(MavenPublication) {
      from components.java
    }

    // Second publication with
    // the name webWar, contains
    // the artifact created by
    // the war task.
    webWar(MavenPublication) {
      from components.web
    }

  }

}
```

Generating POM files

An important part of a Maven publication is the POM file. We already saw that Gradle added a `generatePom<publicationName>` task to our project. Furthermore, we can define some properties of the POM file inside a publication configuration. Gradle also offers a hook to customize the generated POM file even further.

Gradle uses the project's `version`, `group`, and `name` properties in the generated POM file. We create a new example build file where we define the project properties so that they are included in the POM file. The following code shows this:

```
apply plugin: 'maven-publish'
apply plugin: 'java'

// Defined project properties, that are
// used in the generated POM file.
// The name of the project is by default
// the directory name, but we can
// change it via a settings.gradle file
// and the rootProject.name property.
version = '2.1.RELEASE'
group = 'book.gradle'

repositories {
  jcenter()
}

dependencies {
  compile 'org.springframework:spring-context:4.1.4.RELEASE'
}

publishing {
  publications {
    sample(MavenPublication) {
      from components.java
    }
  }
}
```

Now we execute the `generatePomFileForSamplePublication` task. The `pom-default.xml` file is created in the `build/publications/sample` directory. If we open the file, we can see that the `groupId`, `artifactId`, and `version` elements are filled with the values from our Gradle build file. This is shown in the following code:

```
<?xml version="1.0" encoding="UTF-8"?>
<project xsi:schemaLocation="http://maven.apache.org/POM/4.0.0
http://maven.apache.org/xsd/maven-4.0.0.xsd"
xmlns="http://maven.apache.org/POM/4.0.0"
    xmlns:xsi="http://www.w3.org/2001/XMLSchema-instance">
  <modelVersion>4.0.0</modelVersion>
  <groupId>book.gradle</groupId>
  <artifactId>sample</artifactId>
  <version>2.1.RELEASE</version>
  <dependencies>
    <dependency>
      <groupId>org.springframework</groupId>
      <artifactId>spring-context</artifactId>
      <version>4.1.4.RELEASE</version>
      <scope>runtime</scope>
    </dependency>
  </dependencies>
</project>
```

We can override the values for `groupId`, `artifactId`, and `version` inside a publication configuration. We use the `groupId`, `artifactId`, and `version` properties to set values other than the default values taken from the project properties. In the next example build file, we will use these methods to set the values:

```
apply plugin: 'maven-publish'
apply plugin: 'java'

version = '2.1.DEVELOPMENT'
group = 'book.gradle'

repositories {
  jcenter()
}

dependencies {
  compile 'org.springframework:spring-context:4.1.4.RELEASE'
}

publishing {
  publications {
```

```
sample(MavenPublication) {
  groupId = 'book.sample.gradle'
  artifactId ='bookSample'
  version = '2.1'

  from components.java
  }
 }
}
```

Upon executing the `generatePomFileForSamplePublication` task again, we can see the new values in the generated POM file. The following code shows this:

```
<?xml version="1.0" encoding="UTF-8"?>
<project xsi:schemaLocation="http://maven.apache.org/POM/4.0.0
http://maven.apache.org/xsd/maven-4.0.0.xsd"
xmlns="http://maven.apache.org/POM/4.0.0"
    xmlns:xsi="http://www.w3.org/2001/XMLSchema-instance">
  <modelVersion>4.0.0</modelVersion>
  <groupId>book.sample.gradle</groupId>
  <artifactId>bookSample</artifactId>
  <version>2.1</version>
  <dependencies>
    <dependency>
      <groupId>org.springframework</groupId>
      <artifactId>spring-context</artifactId>
      <version>4.1.4.RELEASE</version>
      <scope>runtime</scope>
    </dependency>
  </dependencies>
</project>
```

You may already have noticed that the `generatePomFile<publicationName>Pub lication` task also added a `dependencies` element in the generated POM file. The dependencies of our project are added as runtime dependencies in the POM file. This happens because we use the `from` method with the `components.java` value inside our publication configuration. The Java software component not only adds the `jar` archive tasks as an artifact, but also turns the project dependencies in to Maven runtime dependencies. If we use an archive task to define an artifact, the `dependencies` element is not added to the POM file.

In the following example build file, we use the `artifact` method to define the publication:

```
apply plugin: 'maven-publish'
apply plugin: 'java'

// Defined project properties, that are
// used in the generated POM file.
// The name of the project is by default
// the directory name, but we can
// change it via a settings.gradle file
// and the rootProject.name property.
version = '2.1.RELEASE'
group = 'book.gradle'

repositories {
  jcenter()
}

dependencies {
  compile 'org.springframework:spring-context:4.1.4.RELEASE'
}

publishing {
  publications {
    sample(MavenPublication) {
      artifact jar
    }
  }
}
```

When we run the `generatePomFileForSamplePublication` task from the command line, the POM file is generated. The contents of the POM file are now as follows:

```
<?xml version="1.0" encoding="UTF-8"?>
<project xsi:schemaLocation="http://maven.apache.org/POM/4.0.0
http://maven.apache.org/xsd/maven-4.0.0.xsd"
xmlns="http://maven.apache.org/POM/4.0.0"
    xmlns:xsi="http://www.w3.org/2001/XMLSchema-instance">
  <modelVersion>4.0.0</modelVersion>
  <groupId>book.gradle</groupId>
  <artifactId>sample</artifactId>
  <version>2.1.RELEASE</version>
</project>
```

In the next section, we will learn how we can customize the POM file using a hook. We can then, for example, also change the Maven dependency scope for our project dependencies.

Customizing the POM file

To add some extra elements to the generated POM file, we must use the pom property that is a part of MavenPublication. This returns a MavenPom object, and we can invoke the withXml method from this object to add extra elements to the POM file. We will use a closure with the withXml method to access an XmlProvider object. With the XmlProvider object, we can get a reference to a DOM element with the asElement method, a Groovy node object with the asNode method, or the StringBuilder object with the asString method to extend the POM XML.

In the following example build file, we add the organization and issueMangement elements to the generated POM file:

```
apply plugin: 'maven-publish'
apply plugin: 'java'

version = '2.1.RELEASE'
group = 'book.gradle'

repositories {
  jcenter()
}

dependencies {
  compile 'org.springframework:spring-context:4.1.4.RELEASE'
}

publishing {
  publications {
    sample(MavenPublication) {
      from components.java

      pom.withXml {

        asNode()
          .appendNode('organization')
          .with {
            appendNode('name', 'Gradle')
```

```
            appendNode('url', 'http://www.gradle.org')
        }

    asNode()
      .appendNode('issueManagement')
      .with {
        appendNode('system', 'Jenkins')
        appendNode('url', 'http://buildserver/')
      }
    }
  }
 }
}
```

If we generate the POM file, we can see our newly created elements in the XML version. This is shown in the following code:

```xml
<?xml version="1.0" encoding="UTF-8"?>
<project xmlns="http://maven.apache.org/POM/4.0.0"
xsi:schemaLocation="http://maven.apache.org/POM/4.0.0
http://maven.apache.org/xsd/maven-4.0.0.xsd"
xmlns:xsi="http://www.w3.org/2001/XMLSchema-instance">
  <modelVersion>4.0.0</modelVersion>
  <groupId>book.gradle</groupId>
  <artifactId>sample</artifactId>
  <version>2.1.RELEASE</version>
  <dependencies>
    <dependency>
      <groupId>org.springframework</groupId>
      <artifactId>spring-context</artifactId>
      <version>4.1.4.RELEASE</version>
      <scope>runtime</scope>
    </dependency>
  </dependencies>
  <organization>
    <name>Gradle</name>
    <url>http://www.gradle.org</url>
  </organization>
  <issueManagement>
    <system>Jenkins</system>
    <url>http://buildserver/</url>
  </issueManagement>
</project>
```

In the previous section, we already learned that, if we use the `from` method with the `components.java` value, all project dependencies are added as runtime dependencies in the generated POM file. This might always not be what we want. Using the `withXml` method, not only can we add new elements, we can also change values.

Let's add a hook where we change the runtime scope for dependencies to compile the scope. In the next build file, we will implement this:

```
apply plugin: 'maven-publish'
apply plugin: 'java'

version = '2.1.RELEASE'
group = 'book.gradle'

repositories {
  jcenter()
}

dependencies {
  compile 'org.springframework:spring-context:4.1.4.RELEASE'
}

publishing {
  publications {
    sample(MavenPublication) {
      from components.java

      pom.withXml {
        asNode()
          .dependencies
          .dependency
          .findAll { dependency ->
            // Find all with scope runtime.
            // Could be more specific if we would
            // have more dependencies. For example
            // check group, name and version.
            dependency.scope.text() == 'runtime'
          }
          .each { dependency ->
            // Set scope value to compile.
```

```
                dependency.scope*.value = 'compile'
            }
        }
      }
    }
}
```

The generated POM file now has the following contents:

```xml
<?xml version="1.0" encoding="UTF-8"?>
<project xmlns="http://maven.apache.org/POM/4.0.0"
xsi:schemaLocation="http://maven.apache.org/POM/4.0.0
http://maven.apache.org/xsd/maven-4.0.0.xsd"
xmlns:xsi="http://www.w3.org/2001/XMLSchema-instance">
  <modelVersion>4.0.0</modelVersion>
  <groupId>book.gradle</groupId>
  <artifactId>sample</artifactId>
  <version>2.1.RELEASE</version>
  <dependencies>
    <dependency>
      <groupId>org.springframework</groupId>
      <artifactId>spring-context</artifactId>
      <version>4.1.4.RELEASE</version>
      <scope>compile</scope>
    </dependency>
  </dependencies>
</project>
```

Another solution would be to configure the publication, not with the `from` method but with the `artifact` method. Then, `dependencies` is not added to the POM file because Gradle cannot determine the dependencies for an artifact. Using the `withXml` method, we can add it ourselves based on the project dependencies.

In the following example build file, this solution is implemented:

```
apply plugin: 'maven-publish'
apply plugin: 'java'

version = '2.1.RELEASE'
group = 'book.gradle'

repositories {
  jcenter()
}

dependencies {
```

```
      compile 'org.springframework:spring-context:4.1.4.RELEASE'
}

publishing {
  publications {
    sample(MavenPublication) {
      artifact jar

      pom.withXml {
        // Create dependencies element.
        def dependencies =
          asNode()
            .appendNode('dependencies')

        project
          .configurations['compile']
          .allDependencies
          ?.each { dependency ->

            // Add a dependency element with
            // groupId, artifactId, version and scope,
            // to the dependencies element.
            dependencies.appendNode('dependency').with {
              appendNode('groupId', dependency.group)
              appendNode('artifactId', dependency.name)
              appendNode('version', dependency.version)
              appendNode('scope', 'compile')
            }

          }
      }
    }
  }
}
```

When we invoke the `generatePomFileForSamplePublication` task, we get the following POM file:

```
<?xml version="1.0" encoding="UTF-8"?>
<project xmlns="http://maven.apache.org/POM/4.0.0"
xsi:schemaLocation="http://maven.apache.org/POM/4.0.0
http://maven.apache.org/xsd/maven-4.0.0.xsd"
xmlns:xsi="http://www.w3.org/2001/XMLSchema-instance">
  <modelVersion>4.0.0</modelVersion>
  <groupId>book.gradle</groupId>
```

```
      <artifactId>sample</artifactId>
      <version>2.1.RELEASE</version>
      <dependencies>
        <dependency>
          <groupId>org.springframework</groupId>
          <artifactId>spring-context</artifactId>
          <version>4.1.4.RELEASE</version>
          <scope>compile</scope>
        </dependency>
      </dependencies>
    </project>
```

Defining repositories

We must configure a Maven repository to publish our configured publication. We can choose a local directory or a repository manager, such as Artifactory or Nexus. Gradle also adds support installing the publication to our local Maven repository.

Publishing to the local Maven repository

Gradle already adds our local Maven repository as a destination for our publications. For each named publication, there is a `publish<publicationName>ToMavenLoc al` task. Gradle also creates the `publishToMavenLocal` task, which will publish all publications to the local Maven repository.

We have the following example build file:

```
apply plugin: 'maven-publish'
apply plugin: 'java'

version = '2.1.DEVELOPMENT'
group = 'book.gradle'

repositories {
  jcenter()
}

dependencies {
  compile 'org.springframework:spring-context:4.1.4.RELEASE'
}

publishing {

  publications {
```

```
    publishJar(MavenPublication) {
      artifactId = 'sample'

      from components.java
    }
  }

}
```

From the command line, we will run the `publishToMavenLocal` task and see which tasks are executed:

```
$ gradle publishToMavenLocal
:generatePomFileForPublishJarPublication
:compileJava
:processResources UP-TO-DATE
:classes
:jar
:publishPublishJarPublicationToMavenLocal
:publishToMavenLocal


BUILD SUCCESSFUL


Total time: 5.135 secs
```

You may have noticed that first the publication artifact is created with the `jar` task and its task dependencies. Also, the POM file is generated, and our publication is copied to the local Maven repository via the `publishPublishJarPublicationToMavenLocal` task, which is a task dependency for `publishToMavenLocal`.

When we look at the local Maven repository directory, we see that our project artifact is published:

```
/Users/mrhaki/.m2/repository/
book
└── gradle
    └── sample
        ├── 2.1.RELEASE
        │    ├── sample-2.1.RELEASE.jar
        │    └── sample-2.1.RELEASE.pom
        └── maven-metadata-local.xml
```

Publishing to the Maven repository

If we have our own company's Maven repository or a directory where we want to publish our publications, then we must add it to the `publishing` configuration block. Inside the block, we can add the `repositories` configuration block containing one or more named repositories. For the combination of each publication and repository, Gradle creates a task with the `publish<publicationName>To<repositoryName>Re pository` name pattern.

Next, we will define a simple directory repository in the next example build file with the name `localRepo`:

```
apply plugin: 'maven-publish'
apply plugin: 'java'

version = '2.1.DEVELOPMENT'
group = 'book.gradle'

repositories {
  jcenter()
}

dependencies {
  compile 'org.springframework:spring-context:4.1.4.RELEASE'
}

publishing {

  publications {
    publishJar(MavenPublication) {
      artifactId = 'sample'

      from components.java
    }
  }

  // Add a Maven repository for
  // the publications.
  repositories {
    maven {
      name = 'localRepo'
      url = "$buildDir/localRepo"
    }
  }
}
```

First, we will run the `tasks` task to see which task is added to the `Publishing tasks` group:

```
$ gradle tasks

...

Publishing tasks
----------------

generatePomFileForPublishJarPublication - Generates the Maven POM file
for publication 'publishJar'.

publish - Publishes all publications produced by this project.

publishPublishJarPublicationToLocalRepoRepository - Publishes Maven
publication 'publishJar' to Maven repository 'localRepo'.

publishPublishJarPublicationToMavenLocal - Publishes Maven publication
'publishJar' to the local Maven repository.

publishToMavenLocal - Publishes all Maven publications produced by this
project to the local Maven cache.

...

BUILD SUCCESSFUL


Total time: 4.514 secs
```

To publish our project's artifact, we can execute the `publishPublishJarPublicationToLocalRepoRepository` or `publish` task. The following output shows the tasks that are executed:

```
$ gradle publish

:generatePomFileForPublishJarPublication

:compileJava

:processResources UP-TO-DATE

:classes

:jar

:publishPublishJarPublicationToLocalRepoRepository

Uploading: book/gradle/sample/2.1.DEVELOPMENT/sample-2.1.DEVELOPMENT.jar
to repository remote at file:/Users/mrhaki/Projects/book/sample/build/
localRepo/

Transferring 2K from remote

Uploaded 2K

:publish


BUILD SUCCESSFUL


Total time: 5.012 secs
```

Once the task is performed, we get the following files in the `build/localRepo` directory:

```
build/localRepo/
└── book
    └── gradle
        └── sample
            ├── 2.1.DEVELOPMENT
            │   ├── sample-2.1.DEVELOPMENT.jar
            │   ├── sample-2.1.DEVELOPMENT.jar.md5
            │   ├── sample-2.1.DEVELOPMENT.jar.sha1
            │   ├── sample-2.1.DEVELOPMENT.pom
            │   ├── sample-2.1.DEVELOPMENT.pom.md5
            │   └── sample-2.1.DEVELOPMENT.pom.sha1
            ├── maven-metadata.xml
            ├── maven-metadata.xml.md5
            └── maven-metadata.xml.sha1
```

Publishing to Artifactory

To publish our publications to an Artifactory repository with a Maven layout, we only have to configure the repository in the `publications.repositories` configuration block. We can set the `url` property, a `name`, and optional security credentials.

In the next example build file, we use an Artifactory repository to which we publish the publication:

```
apply plugin: 'maven-publish'
apply plugin: 'java'

version = '2.1.DEVELOPMENT'
group = 'book.gradle'

repositories {
  jcenter()
}

dependencies {
```

```
        compile 'org.springframework:spring-context:4.1.4.RELEASE'
    }

    publishing {

        publications {
            publishJar(MavenPublication) {
                artifactId = 'sample'

                from components.java
            }
        }

        // Add a Artifactory repository for
        // the publications with Maven layout.
        repositories {
            maven {
                name = 'artifactory'
                url = "http://localhost:8081/artifactory/libs-release-local"

                // Username and password should be
                // saved outside build file in
                // real life, eg. in gradle.properties
                // or passed via command line as
                // project properties.
                credentials {
                    username = 'user'
                    password = 'passw0rd'
                }
            }
        }
    }
```

Gradle creates a new publishPublishJarPublicationToArtifactoryRepository task based on the publication name and the repository name. When we invoke the task, we can see that the publication is deployed to the Artifactory repository. The following code shows this:

```
$ gradle publishPublishJarPublicationToArtifactoryRepository
:generatePomFileForPublishJarPublication
:compileJava
:processResources UP-TO-DATE
:classes
:jar
```

```
:publishPublishJarPublicationToArtifactoryRepository
```

Uploading: book/gradle/sample/2.1.DEVELOPMENT/sample-2.1.DEVELOPMENT.jar
to repository remote at http://localhost:8081/artifactory/libs-release-
local

Transferring 2K from remote

Uploaded 2K

BUILD SUCCESSFUL

Total time: 5.012 secs

When we open the Artifactory web application in a web browser, we can see that our project is now part of the repository, as shown in the following screenshot:

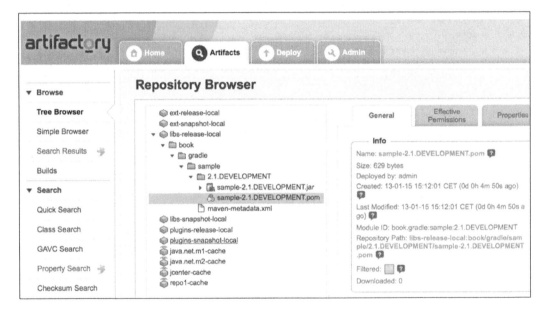

Publishing to Nexus

Another repository manager is Nexus. Publishing to a Nexus repository manager is not much different than publishing to Artifactory or a local directory. We only have to change the `url` property to reference the repository and set the optional security credentials.

In the following example build file, we use a Nexus repository manager:

```
apply plugin: 'maven-publish'
apply plugin: 'java'

version = '2.1.DEVELOPMENT'
group = 'book.gradle'

repositories {
  jcenter()
}

dependencies {
  compile 'org.springframework:spring-context:4.1.4.RELEASE'
}

publishing {

  publications {
    publishJar(MavenPublication) {
      artifactId = 'sample'

      from components.java
    }
  }

  // Add a Maven repository for
  // the publications.
  repositories {
    maven {
      name = 'nexus'
      url = "http://localhost:8081/nexus/content/repositories/
releases"
      credentials {
        username = 'admin'
        password = 'admin123'
      }
    }
  }
}
```

This time, the `publishPublishJarPublicationToNexusRepository` task is created. The task is also added as a task dependency to the `publish` task. To accomplish this, use the following code:

```
$ gradle publishPublishJarPublicationToNexusRepository
:generatePomFileForPublishJarPublication
:compileJava
:processResources UP-TO-DATE
:classes
:jar
:publishPublishJarPublicationToNexusRepository
Uploading: book/gradle/sample/2.1.DEVELOPMENT/sample-2.1.DEVELOPMENT.jar
to repository remote at http://localhost:8081/nexus/content/repositories/
releases
Transferring 2K from remote
Uploaded 2K


BUILD SUCCESSFUL


Total time: 5.012 secs
```

When we take a look with the Nexus web application inside the repository, we can see that our project is added to the repository, as shown in the following screenshot:

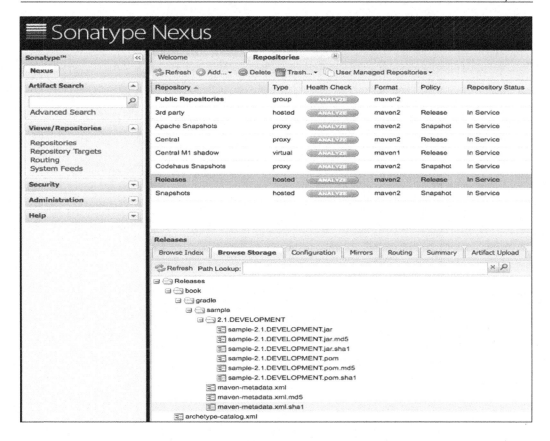

Summary

In this chapter, you learned how to use the new and developing `maven-publish` plugin. You saw how you can declare your publications with the `publications` configuration block. Gradle will automatically create new tasks based on what you declared as publications.

You also learned how to customize the POM file that is generated by the Gradle publishing tasks.

Finally, you saw how you can configure Maven repositories so you can deploy your publications to them. We configured a local directory, which could also be a network share, and showed you how to configure an Artifactory or Nexus repository manager.

In the next chapter, you will see how you can upload to Bintray.

6
Publishing to Bintray

In the previous chapter, we learned how to deploy our artifacts to a Maven repository. In this chapter, you will learn how we can deploy our artifacts to Bintray as a Maven repository. We will see what Bintray is and how it helps to publish our project.

We will see how we can configure the Gradle Bintray plugin to deploy our artifacts.

What is Bintray?

Bintray advertises itself as a Distribution as a Service. This means that when we have something we want to distribute, for example our project artifacts, we can use Bintray. Bintray offers a platform to store the software we want to share and makes it accessible for others to download. Around this, there is a lot of tooling to provide insights into how the packages are distributed and used. Bintray also offers a REST API to make it easy to work with the platform. The company running Bintray is JFrog, which is very well known for its repository product, Artifactory.

A part of Bintray is called JCenter. JCenter hosts Java dependencies within the Bintray platform. We already learned about JCenter as a repository host for dependencies. However, we can also use JCenter as a distribution repository for our own dependencies. In this chapter, we are going to use JCenter to deploy our artifacts.

Defining a new repository

Before we can use Bintray's JCenter, we must create an account with Bintray at
`https://bintray.com`. One of the easiest ways is to use your existing GitHub
account to sign in.

Next, we will create a new repository in which we will store our artifacts. So, first
we log in to Bintray. From our user page, we will select the **New repository** option.
In our browser window, we can see some fields we need to fill in, as shown in the
following screenshot:

We need to give our repository a name and an optional description. We choose **Maven** as the type of repository. Bintray can also be used for other types of dependencies, but for our Java code we want to use Maven. After we have filled in all the fields, we click on the **Create** button, and Bintray creates a new and empty repository. In the next screenshot, we will see our newly created repository:

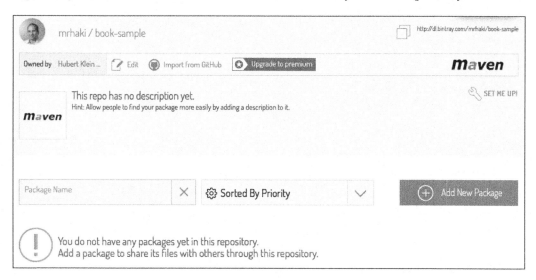

Defining the Bintray plugin

In order to deploy our artifacts to JCenter, we use the Bintray Gradle plugin. This plugin adds extra functionality to our project to publish our artifacts.

Let's continue with our example build file from the previous project. The build file is for a Java project with some code. We will use the publishing plugin to define our publications or artifacts for the project. We will now add the Gradle plugin to the project by using the `buildscript` configuration block. In the next example build file, we will apply the Bintray plugin to our project. The following code shows this:

```
// Define Bintray plugin.
buildscript {
  repositories {
    jcenter()
  }

  dependencies {
```

```
        classpath 'com.jfrog.bintray.gradle:gradle-bintray-plugin:1.1
    }
}

// Apply plugin to project.
apply plugin: 'com.jfrog.bintray'

apply plugin: 'maven-publish'
apply plugin: 'java'

version = '1.0.RELEASE'
group = 'book.gradle'

repositories {
    jcenter()
}

dependencies {
    compile 'org.springframework:spring-context:4.1.4.RELEASE'
}

publishing {
    publications {
        sample(MavenPublication) {
            from components.java
        }
    }
}
```

Since the release of Gradle 2.1, we use an alternative syntax to include an external plugin in our build script. The new syntax works for plugins that are deployed to the Gradle plugin portal. The feature is incubating, which means it can change in the future. Also, an important restriction is that the new syntax is not supported in the subprojects and allprojects configuration blocks. In the following example build file, the new syntax to add a plugin is used:

```
// Define and apply Bintray plugin.
plugins {
    id 'com.jfrog.bintray' version '1.0'
}
```

With the new plugin in our project, we can run the `tasks` command to see which tasks have been added by the plugin:

```
$ gradle tasks

...

Publishing tasks
----------------

bintrayUpload - Publishes artifacts to bintray.com.

...
```

We notice the `bintrayUpload` task that has been added by the plugin to our project.

Deploying publications to Bintray

Before we can run the `bintrayUpload` task, we must add some configuration to our Gradle build file. The Bintray plugin can be configured with the `bintray` configuration block. Inside this configuration block, we see all the properties needed to deploy our project's publications to Bintray.

First, we need to set the username and the API key for the Bintray account we are using to deploy with. To get the API key, we must first log in to Bintray in our web browser. From our account page, we click on the **Edit** button. Next, we will select the **API** menu option to get to our API key. The key can then be copied to the clipboard so that we can use it in our build script. The `user` and `key` properties from the `bintray` configuration block contain information that we don't want to share. It is best to keep the values of these properties externalized from our Gradle build file. We can add a `gradle.properties` file to our project directory with the values for the properties. The `gradle.properties` file can also be added to our Gradle user home directory, which, by default, is `<user_home>/.gradle`. Alternatively, we can use the command-line options `-P` and `--project-prop` to set the values.

The `user` and `key` properties are required. Also, we must set the `pkg.repo` properties with the repository name we have in Bintray and `pkg.name` as the group name of our deployment. Finally, we need to define what we need to publish. Fortunately, the Bintray plugin supports the Gradle publishing plugin, so we can reuse the publication we have configured in the build file.

In the following example build file, we configure the Bintray plugin in the `bintray` configuration block:

```
// Define Bintray plugin.
buildscript {
  repositories {
```

```
      jcenter()
  }

  dependencies {
    classpath 'com.jfrog.bintray.gradle:gradle-bintray-plugin:1.0'
  }
}

// Apply plugin to project.
apply plugin: 'com.jfrog.bintray'

apply plugin: 'maven-publish'
apply plugin: 'java'

version = '1.0.RELEASE'
group = 'book.gradle'

repositories {
  jcenter()
}

dependencies {
  compile 'org.springframework:spring-context:4.1.4.RELEASE'
}

publishing {
  publications {
    sample(MavenPublication) {
      from components.java
    }
  }
}

bintray {

  // Use externalized project property bintrayUsername.
  user = bintrayUsername

  // Use externalized project property bintrayApiKey.
  key = bintrayApiKey

  // Define publication that needs to be published
  // to Bintray.
```

```
publications = ['sample']

pkg {
  // Name of repository in Bintray
  repo = 'book-sample'

  // Name for package.
  name = 'sample'
}

}
```

Before we can upload our artifact, we must first create a `book-sample` repository with the `sample` package by using the web browser interface of Bintray. We need to log in using our account and then select the **New repository** link. In the following screenshot, we see the fields that need to be filled in:

After we have created a new repository, we get an overview of the repository, as shown in the following screenshot:

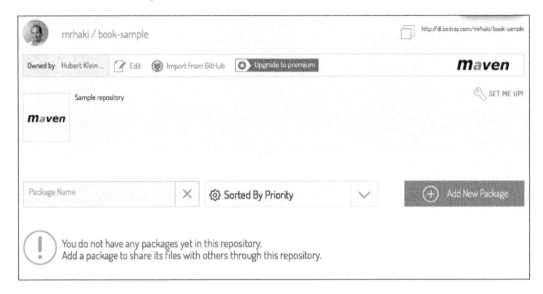

From this screen, we click on the **New package** button. A repository can contain multiple packages. The next screenshot shows the fields that we need to fill to create a new package. We must set the **Name**, the **Licenses** field, and a **Version control** link.

Create New Package

Package Details

Package avatar

⬡   ⬆ Upload a file

Name*

[   ]

Description

[   ]

Licenses *

[Start typing to see available license types]

Request a new license type

Tags

[Enter comma-separated description tags]

Website

[   ]

Issues tracker

[   ]

Version control *

[   ]

☐   Make download numbers in stats public

[Create Package]   ⓧ Cancel

Once we have created the package in our repository, we can invoke the `bintrayUpload` task for our project. Let's see the output when we invoke the task:

```
$ gradle bintrayUpload
:generatePomFileForSamplePublication
:compileJava
:processResources UP-TO-DATE
:classes
:jar
:publishSamplePublicationToMavenLocal
:bintrayUpload


BUILD SUCCESSFUL


Total time: 9.125 secs
```

We notice that the `bintrayUpload` task is dependent on the tasks necessary to first compile and build our artifact before it is uploaded. We do not have to define this task dependency ourselves.

Everything was built successfully, so we can now open our web browser and go to the repository and package page. In the following screenshot, we see our updated package web page:

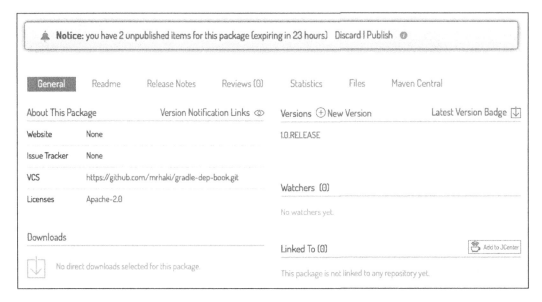

Bintray first puts the uploaded files into an unpublished state. This way, we have time to decide whether we really want to publish this version or not. We can see the message on our screen. We are sure that we want to publish this version, so we will click on the **Publish** link. Now, the files are published so that others can also see the files. If we click on the release version, we can even see the actual files in our web browser. The following screenshot shows our published artifact JAR file and the corresponding POM file:

Configuring the Bintray plugin

We have configured the required configuration properties to get our project published to Bintray. However, the plugin allows for more configuration. We can see the configuration properties in the following table:

Name	Description
user	This sets the Bintray username.
key	This sets the API key.
configurations	This defines the configuration list with deployable files.
publications	This defines the list of publications to be deployed.
filesSpec	Use CopySpec to define the arbitrary files to be published, which are not part of a publication or configuration.

Name	Description
dryRun	This allows you to execute all tasks without deploying them.
publish	Should version be published after upload, instead of publishing it via the web browser.
pkg.repo	This is the name of the repository.
pkg.name	This is the name of the package.
pkg.userOrg	This is the optional organization name when the repository belongs to an organization.
pkg.desc	This is the description of the package.
pkg.websiteUrl	This is the URL of the website belonging to the project.
pkg.issueTrackerUrl	This is the URL of the issue-tracking system used for the project.
pkg.vcsUrl	This is the URL of the version control system used.
pkg.licenses	This is the list of licenses valid for this project.
pkg.labels	This is the list of labels describing what the project is about.
pkg.publicDownloadNumbers	This shows how many times published files are downloaded.
pkg.attributes	This is the map of custom attributes for package.
pkg.version.name	This is the custom Bintray version.
pkg.version.desc	This is the description specific to this version.
pkg.version.released	This is the date of release.
pkg.version.vcsTag	This is the tag for this version in the version control system.
pkg.version.attributes	These are the custom attributes for this version package.
pkg.version.gpg.sign	This is set to true to use GPG signing.
pkg.version.gpg.passphrase	This is the passphrase for GPG signing.
pkg.version.mavenCentralSync.sync	This is set to true to sync with Maven Central.
pkg.version.mavenCentralSync.user	This is the user token to sync with Maven Central.
pkg.version.mavenCentralSync.password	This is the password for the user syncing with Maven Central.
pkg.version.mavenCentralSync.close	By default, the staging repository is closed and artifacts are released to Maven Central. You can optionally turn this behavior off (by putting 0 as value) and release the version manually.

In the following example build file, we will use some of these configuration properties:

```
// Define Bintray plugin.
buildscript {
  repositories {
    jcenter()
  }

  dependencies {
    classpath 'com.jfrog.bintray.gradle:gradle-bintray-plugin:1.0'
  }
}

// Apply plugin to project.
apply plugin: 'com.jfrog.bintray'

apply plugin: 'maven-publish'
apply plugin: 'java'

version = '1.0.2.RELEASE'
group = 'book.gradle'

repositories {
  jcenter()
}

dependencies {
  compile 'org.springframework:spring-context:4.1.4.RELEASE'
}

publishing {
  publications {
    sample(MavenPublication) {
      from components.java
    }
  }
}

bintray {
  user = bintrayUsername
  key = bintrayApiKey
```

```
    publications = ['sample']

    publish = true

    pkg {
      repo = 'book-sample'
      name = 'full-sample'

      desc = 'Sample package for Gradle book.'

      websiteUrl = 'https://github.com/mrhaki/gradle-dep-book/'
      issueTrackerUrl = 'https://github.com/mrhaki/gradle-dep-
      book/issues'
      vcsUrl = 'https://github.com/mrhaki/gradle-dep-book.git'

      licenses = ['Apache-2.0']

      labels = ['book', 'sample', 'Gradle']

      publicDownloadNumbers = true

      version {
        desc = 'Fixed some issues.'
        released = new Date()
      }

    }

  }
```

It is good to see that if we define the vcsUrl and licenses configuration properties, the plugin will automatically create the package in our repository. So, we don't have to use the web browser to create a new package. Instead, we can use the configuration in our build script to automatically create a package. Also, notice that the package is automatically published, unlike in the first example in which it was in an unpublished state.

Summary

In this chapter, you learned how to use the third-party Bintray plugin. We learned about Bintray and JCenter. We saw how we can create a repository on Bintray and use it to deploy our project as a package to this repository.

You learned about the different configuration properties that can be set for the deployment to Bintray.

In the next chapter, we will see how we can upload to an Ivy repository.

7
Publishing to an Ivy Repository

You learned in a previous chapter how we can publish our project artifacts to a Maven repository. In this chapter, we are going to use an Ivy repository to which we can publish.

Just as with publishing to a Maven repository, we are going to use the new and incubating publishing feature in Gradle to publish to an Ivy repository.

Defining publications

We must add the `ivy-publish` plugin to our project to be able to publish our artifacts to an Ivy repository. The plugin allows us to use the Ivy format to describe our artifacts that need to be published.

The `ivy-publish` plugin is based on the general `publishing` plugin. The `publishing` plugin adds a new `publishing` extension to our project. We can use a `publications` configuration block in our build script to configure the artifacts we want to publish and the repositories we want to deploy to. The `publications` extension has the `PublishingExtension` type in the `org.gradle.api.publish` package. The plugin also adds a general life cycle `publish` task to the project. Other tasks can be added as task dependencies to this task, so with a single `publish` task, all the project's publications can be published.

The `ivy-publish` plugins also adds some extra task rules to the project. There is a task to generate an Ivy descriptor file to each publication in the project. The plugins also add a task rule based on a combination of the publication and the repository to publish a publication to the specified repository.

Let's create an example build file and apply the `ivy-publish` plugin to see the new task:

```
apply plugin: 'ivy-publish'
apply plugin: 'java'
```

Now, we will invoke the `tasks` task from the command line:

```
$ gradle tasks

...

Publishing tasks
----------------

publish - Publishes all publications produced by this project.

...

BUILD SUCCESSFUL


Total time: 4.589 secs
```

In the output, we see the `publish` task. The dynamic task rules to publish single publications to repositories are not shown.

To configure our publications, we must first add a `publishing` configuration block. Inside the block, we will define the `publications` configuration block. In this block, we define a publication. A publication defines what needs to be published. The `ivy-publish` plugin expects that a publication of the `IvyPublication` type is found in the `org.gradle.api.publish.ivy` package. Besides the artifacts that need to be published, we can also define details for the generated Ivy descriptor file.

Defining publication artifacts

A publication we define must have a unique name in our project. We can add multiple publications with their own name inside a `publications` configuration block. To add an artifact, we can use the `artifact` method in the publication definition. We can also use the `artifacts` property to directly set all artifacts.

We can define the artifact with the `artifact` method in the ways described in the following table:

Type	Description
AbstractArchiveTask	The information for the artifact is extracted from the archive task. The artifact is an instance of `PublishArtifact` in the `org.gradle.api.artifacts` package.
File	The information for the artifact is extracted from the filename.
Map	This is another way to define artifacts. The map must contain a `source` key referencing a file or archive task and other properties we can use, such as `classifier` and `extension`, to further configure the artifact.

Using archive task artifacts

In the following example build file, we define a new publication with the `publishJar` name and we define the output of the `jar` archive task as an artifact:

```
apply plugin: 'ivy-publish'
apply plugin: 'java'

// Configuration block for publishing
// artifacts from the project.
publishing {

  // Define publications with what
  // needs to be published.
  publications {

    // Name of this publication
    // is publishJar.
    publishJar(IvyPublication) {

      // Use output of jar task
      // as the artifact for
      // the publication.
      artifact jar

      // Alternatively we can use
```

```
        // a Map notation:
        // artifact source: jar
    }


    }
}
```

Next, we run the `tasks` task, and in the output, we see new generated tasks to publish this publication:

```
$ gradle tasks

...

Publishing tasks
----------------

generateDescriptorFileForPublishJarPublication - Generates the Ivy Module
Descriptor XML file for publication 'publishJar'.

publish - Publishes all publications produced by this project.

...

BUILD SUCCESSFUL


Total time: 4.215 secs
```

Notice the extra task, `generateDescriptorFileForPublishJarPublication`. The name of the `publishJar` publication is used for this task. Gradle uses the following pattern for a task to generate an Ivy descriptor XML file for a `generateDescriptorF ileFor<publicationName>Publication` publication. We cannot yet invoke the task because we also need to set the `group` and `version` project properties, but we will see this in the section about generating an Ivy descriptor file. We will now focus on defining the artifacts for a publication in this section.

We are not restricted to one artifact for a publication; we can add more by invoking the `artifact` method multiple times. We can even use the `artifacts` property to assign multiple artifacts. It is important that each artifact has unique `classifier` and `extension` property values for a single publication. Gradle will check this before we can invoke any tasks, so we immediately get an error message when the artifacts don't have a unique combination of `classifier` and `extensions` property values.

In the following example build file, we add two extra artifacts to our publication with the `artifact` method:

```
apply plugin: 'ivy-publish'
apply plugin: 'java'

task sourcesJar(type: Jar) {
```

```
    from sourceSets.main.allJava
    classifier = 'sources'
}


task javadocJar(type: Jar) {
    from javadoc
}


publishing {

    publications {

        publishJar(IvyPublication) {

            artifact jar

            // Add output of sourcesJar task
            // as an artifacts. In the task
            // the classifier is already
            // set to sources.
            artifact sourcesJar

            artifact javadocJar {
                // Each artifact must have
                // a unique classifier.
                // We can set the classifier
                // via the task as in sourcesJar
                // or here in the artifact configuration.
                classifier = 'javadoc'
            }

            // Or with a Map notation we
            // can write:
            // artifact source: javadocJar, classifier: 'javadoc'

        }

    }
}
```

Instead of using the `artifact` method, we can also use the `artifacts` property and assign multiple artifacts. Each of the artifacts we assign must have a unique combination of `classifier` and `extension` property values. In the next example build file, we will use the same artifacts as in the previous example, but this time, we will assign them to the `artifacts` property:

```
apply plugin: 'ivy-publish'
apply plugin: 'java'

task sourcesJar(type: Jar) {
  from sourceSets.main.allJava
  classifier = 'sources'
}

task javadocJar(type: Jar) {
  from javadoc
  classifier = 'javadoc'
}

publishing {

  publications {

    publishJar(IvyPublication) {

      // Use artifacts property to
      // define the artifacts.
      // The classifier for each of
      // these artifacts must be
      // unique.
      artifacts = [
        jar,
        sourcesJar,
        javaDocJar]

    }

  }
}
```

Using file artifacts

Instead of an archive task, we can also use a file as an artifact. Gradle tries to extract the `extension` and `classifier` properties from the filename. We can also configure these properties ourselves when we add the file as a publication artifact.

In the following example build file, we use the `src/files/README` and `src/files/COPYRIGHT` files as a publication artifact:

```
apply plugin: 'ivy-publish'

publishing {
  publications {
    documentation(IvyPublication) {

      // Use file name as a publication artifact.
      artifact 'src/files/README'

      artifact('src/files/COPYRIGHT') {
        // Each file artifact must have a
        // unique classifier and extension.
        classifier = 'metaInformation'
      }

      // Alternative syntax is with
      // the Map notation:
      // artifact source: 'src/files/README'
      // artifact source: 'src/files/COPYRIGHT',
      //            extension: 'metaInformation'

    }
  }
}
```

Using software components

Besides the `artifact` method and the `artifacts` property, we can also use the `from` method inside a `publications` configuration block. We specify a Gradle `SoftwareComponent` object as an argument to the `from` method. The `java` plugin adds a `SoftwareComponent` object with the name `java`, and it includes the `jar` artifact and all runtime dependencies. The `war` plugin adds the `war` artifact as a `SoftwareComponent` object.

In the next example build file, we will apply the `war` plugin to our project. The `war` plugin extends the `java` plugin, so we will also implicitly apply the `java` plugin to our project. We will also define two publications, with each using the `SoftwareComponent` object from both plugins:

```
apply plugin: 'ivy-publish'
apply plugin: 'war'


publishing {

  publications {

    // First publication with
    // the name javaJar, contains
    // the artifact created by the
    // jar task.
    javaJar(IvyPublication) {
      from components.java
    }

    // Second publication with
    // the name webWar, contains
    // the artifact created by
    // the war task.
    webWar(IvyPublication) {
      from components.web
    }

  }

}
```

Generating Ivy descriptor files

An important part of an Ivy publication is the descriptor file. We already saw that Gradle added a `generateDescriptorFile<publicationName>` task to our project. Furthermore, we can define some properties of the descriptor file inside a publication configuration. Gradle also offers a hook to customize the generated descriptor file even further.

Gradle uses the project's `version`, `group`, `name`, and `status` properties for the `info` element in the Ivy descriptor file generated. We will create a new example build file where we define the project properties, so they will be included in the file:

```
apply plugin: 'ivy-publish'
apply plugin: 'java'

// Defined project properties, that are
// used in the generated descriptor file.
// The name of the project is by default
// the directory name, but we can
// change it via a settings.gradle file
// and the rootProject.name property.
version = '2.1.RELEASE'
group = 'book.gradle'

repositories {
  jcenter()
}

dependencies {
  compile 'org.springframework:spring-context:4.1.4.RELEASE'
}

publishing {
  publications {
    sample(IvyPublication) {
      from components.java
    }
  }
}
```

Now, we execute the `generateDescriptorFileForSamplePublication` task. An `ivy.xml` file is created in the `build/publications/sample` directory. If we open the file, we can see that the `info` element attributes are filled with the values from our Gradle build file. The following code shows this:

```
<?xml version="1.0" encoding="UTF-8"?>
<ivy-module version="2.0">
  <info organisation="book.gradle" module="sample"
  revision="2.1.RELEASE" status="integration"
  publication="20150424051601"/>
  <configurations>
    <conf name="default" visibility="public" extends="runtime"/>
    <conf name="runtime" visibility="public"/>
```

```
    </configurations>
    <publications>
      <artifact name="sample" type="jar" ext="jar" conf="runtime"/>
    </publications>
    <dependencies>
      <dependency org="org.springframework" name="spring-context"
      rev="4.1.4.RELEASE" conf="runtime-&gt;default"/>
    </dependencies>
  </ivy-module>
```

We can override the values for `organisation`, `module`, `revision`, `status`, and `branch` inside a publication configuration. We need to set the properties in the configuration block of `IvyPublication`. The `status` and `branch` properties need to be set via the `descriptor` property. Via the `descriptor` property, we can also add new child elements to the `info` element in the Ivy descriptor file. In the next example build file, we will use these methods to set the values:

```
apply plugin: 'ivy-publish'
apply plugin: 'java'

version = '2.1.DEVELOPMENT'
group = 'book.gradle'

repositories {
  jcenter()
}

dependencies {
  compile 'org.springframework:spring-context:4.1.4.RELEASE'
}

publishing {
  publications {
    sample(IvyPublication) {
      organisation = 'book.sample.gradle'
      module ='bookSample'
      version = '2.1'
      descriptor.status = 'published'
      descriptor.branch = 'n/a'

      // Add extra element as child
```

```
        // for info.
        descriptor.extraInfo '', 'ivyauthor', 'Hubert Klein
        Ikkink'

        from components.java
    }
  }
}
```

We execute the `generateDescriptorFileForSamplePublication` task again,
as shown in the following code, and we see the new values in the generated Ivy
descriptor file:

```xml
<?xml version="1.0" encoding="UTF-8"?>
<ivy-module version="2.0">
  <info organisation="book.sample.gradle" module="bookSample"
  branch="n/a" revision="2.1.DEVELOPMENT" status="published"
  publication="20150424053039">
    <ns:ivyauthor xmlns:ns="">Hubert Klein Ikkink</ns:ivyauthor>
  </info>
  <configurations>
    <conf name="default" visibility="public" extends="runtime"/>
    <conf name="runtime" visibility="public"/>
  </configurations>
  <publications>
    <artifact name="bookSample" type="jar" ext="jar"
    conf="runtime"/>
  </publications>
  <dependencies>
    <dependency org="org.springframework" name="spring-context"
    rev="4.1.4.RELEASE" conf="runtime-&gt;default"/>
  </dependencies>
</ivy-module>
```

The dependencies of our project are added as dependencies in the generated
descriptor file. This happens because we use the `from` method with the `components.`
`java` value inside our publication configuration. The Java software component not
only adds the `jar` archive tasks as an artifact, but also turns the project dependencies
into dependencies in the descriptor file. If we use an archive task to define an artifact,
the `dependencies` element is not added to the file.

In the following example build file, we use the `artifact` method to define the publication:

```
apply plugin: 'ivy-publish'
apply plugin: 'java'

// Defined project properties, that are
// used in the generated descriptor file.
// The name of the project is by default
// the directory name, but we can
// change it via a settings.gradle file
// and the rootProject.name property.
version = '2.1.RELEASE'
group = 'book.gradle'

repositories {
  jcenter()
}

dependencies {
  compile 'org.springframework:spring-context:4.1.4.RELEASE'
}

publishing {
  publications {
    sample(IvyPublication) {
      artifact jar
    }
  }
}
```

When we run the `generateDescriptorFileForSamplePublication` task from the command line, the Ivy descriptor file is generated. The contents of the file are now as follows:

```
<?xml version="1.0" encoding="UTF-8"?>
<ivy-module version="2.0">
  <info organisation="book.gradle" module="sample"
  revision="2.1.RELEASE" status="integration"
  publication="20150424053351"/>
  <configurations/>
  <publications>
    <artifact name="sample" type="jar" ext="jar"/>
  </publications>
  <dependencies/>
</ivy-module>
```

In the next section, you will learn how we can customize the descriptor using the withXml method of the descriptor property. We can then, for example, also change the dependency scope of our project dependencies.

Customizing the descriptor file

To add extra elements to the generated file, we must use the descriptor property that is part of IvyPublication. This returns an IvyModuleDescriptorSpec object, and we will invoke the withXml method from this object to add extra elements to the descriptor file. We use a closure with the withXml method to access an XmlProvider object. With the XmlProvider object, we can get a reference to a DOM element with the asElement method, a Groovy node object with the asNode method, or a StringBuilder object with the asString method to extend the descriptor XML.

In the following example build file, we add the description and issueMangement elements to the generated descriptor file:

```
apply plugin: 'ivy-publish'
apply plugin: 'java'

version = '2.1.RELEASE'
group = 'book.gradle'

repositories {
  jcenter()
}

dependencies {
  compile 'org.springframework:spring-context:4.1.4.RELEASE'
}

publishing {
  publications {
    sample(IvyPublication) {
      from components.java

      // Customize generated descriptor XML.
      descriptor.withXml {

        asNode()
          .appendNode('description',
              'Sample Gradle project')

        asNode()
```

```
                .appendNode('issueManagement')
                .with {
                  appendNode('system', 'Jenkins')
                  appendNode('url', 'http://buildserver/')
                }
            }
          }
        }
      }
```

If we generate the Ivy descriptor file, we can see our newly created elements in the XML version:

```xml
<?xml version="1.0" encoding="UTF-8"?>
<ivy-module version="2.0">
  <info organisation="book.gradle" module="sample"
  revision="2.1.RELEASE" status="integration"
  publication="20150424053914"/>
  <configurations>
    <conf name="default" visibility="public" extends="runtime"/>
    <conf name="runtime" visibility="public"/>
  </configurations>
  <publications>
    <artifact name="sample" type="jar" ext="jar" conf="runtime"/>
  </publications>
  <dependencies>
    <dependency org="org.springframework" name="spring-context"
    rev="4.1.4.RELEASE" conf="runtime-&gt;default"/>
  </dependencies>
  <description>Sample Gradle project</description>
  <issueManagement>
    <system>Jenkins</system>
    <url>http://buildserver/</url>
  </issueManagement>
</ivy-module>
```

In the previous section, you already learned that if we use the `from` method with the `components.java` value, all project dependencies are added as runtime dependencies in the generated descriptor file. This might not be what we always want. Using the `withXml` method, we can not only add new elements, but also change values.

Let's add a hook where we change the module attribute of the info element. In the next build file, we will implement this:

```
apply plugin: 'ivy-publish'
apply plugin: 'java'

version = '2.1.RELEASE'
group = 'book.gradle'

repositories {
  jcenter()
}

dependencies {
  compile 'org.springframework:spring-context:4.1.4.RELEASE'
}

publishing {
  publications {
    sample(IvyPublication) {
      from components.java

      descriptor.withXml {
        // Replace value for module attribute
        // in info element.
        new StringBuilder(
          asString()
            .replaceAll(
              /module="sample"/,
              'module="ivyChapter"'))
      }
    }
  }
}
```

The generated descriptor file now has the following contents:

```
<?xml version="1.0" encoding="UTF-8"?>
<ivy-module version="2.0">
  <info organisation="book.gradle" module="ivyChapter"
  revision="2.1.RELEASE" status="integration"
  publication="20150424055754"/>
  <configurations>
    <conf name="default" visibility="public" extends="runtime"/>
    <conf name="runtime" visibility="public"/>
```

```
    </configurations>
    <publications>
      <artifact name="sample" type="jar" ext="jar" conf="runtime"/>
    </publications>
    <dependencies>
      <dependency org="org.springframework" name="spring-context"
      rev="4.1.4.RELEASE" conf="runtime-&gt;default"/>
    </dependencies>
  </ivy-module>
```

Defining repositories

We must configure an Ivy repository to publish our configured publication. We can choose a local directory or a repository manager, such as Artifactory or Nexus.

Publishing to a local directory

If we have a directory where we want to publish our publications, we must add it to the publishing configuration block. Inside the block, we add a repositories configuration block containing one or more named repositories. For the combination of each publication and repository, Gradle creates a task with the publish<publicationName>To<repositoryName>Repository name pattern.

We define a simple directory repository in the next example build file with the name localRepo:

```
apply plugin: 'ivy-publish'
apply plugin: 'java'

version = '2.1.DEVELOPMENT'
group = 'book.gradle'

repositories {
  jcenter()
}

dependencies {
  compile 'org.springframework:spring-context:4.1.4.RELEASE'
}

publishing {

  publications {
    publishJar(IvyPublication) {
```

```
        module = 'sample'

        from components.java
      }
    }

    // Add a local director as repository
    // for the publications.
    repositories {
      ivy {
        name = 'localRepo'
        url = "$buildDir/localRepo"
      }
    }
  }
```

First, we run the `tasks` task to see which task is added to the `Publishing tasks` group:

```
$ gradle tasks
...
Publishing tasks
----------------
generateDescriptorFileForPublishJarPublication - Generates the Ivy Module
Descriptor XML file for publication 'publishJar'.

publish - Publishes all publications produced by this project.

publishPublishJarPublicationToLocalRepoRepository - Publishes Ivy
publication 'publishJar' to Ivy repository 'localRepo'.
...
BUILD SUCCESSFUL

Total time: 11.514 secs
```

To publish our project's artifact, we can execute the
`publishPublishJarPublicationToLocalRepoRepository` or `publish` tasks. The
following output shows the tasks that are executed:

```
$ gradle publish
:generateDescriptorFileForPublishJarPublication
:compileJava
:processResources UP-TO-DATE
:classes
```

```
:jar
:publishPublishJarPublicationToLocalRepoRepository
:publish

BUILD SUCCESSFUL

Total time: 6.383 secs
```

Once the task has been run, we get the following files in the `build/localRepo` directory:

```
build/localRepo/
└── book.gradle
    └── sample
        └── 2.1.DEVELOPMENT
            ├── ivy-2.1.DEVELOPMENT.xml
            ├── ivy-2.1.DEVELOPMENT.xml.sha1
            ├── sample-2.1.DEVELOPMENT.jar
            └── sample-2.1.DEVELOPMENT.jar.sha1
```

Publishing to Artifactory

To publish our publications to an Artifactory repository, we only have to configure the repository in the `publications.repositories` configuration block. We can set the `url` property, a `name`, and optional security credentials.

In the next example build file, we will use an Artifactory repository to publish the publication to:

```
apply plugin: 'ivy-publish'
apply plugin: 'java'

version = '2.1.DEVELOPMENT'
group = 'book.gradle'

repositories {
  jcenter()
}

dependencies {
```

```
      compile 'org.springframework:spring-context:4.1.4.RELEASE'
   }

   publishing {

     publications {
       publishJar(IvyPublication) {
         module = 'sample'

         from components.java
       }
     }

     // Add a Artifactory repository for
     // the publications with Maven layout.
     repositories {
       ivy {
         name = 'artifactory'
         url = "http://localhost:8081/artifactory/libs-release-
         local"

         // Username and password should be
         // saved outside build file in
         // real life, eg. in gradle.properties.
         credentials {
           username = 'user'
           password = 'passw0rd'
         }
       }
     }
   }
```

Gradle creates a new task,
`publishPublishJarPublicationToArtifactoryRepository`, based on
the publication name and the repository name. When we invoke the task,
we can see that the publication is deployed to the Artifactory repository,
as shown in the following code:

```
$ gradle publishPublishJarPublicationToArtifactoryRepository
:generateDescriptorFileForPublishJarPublication
:compileJava UP-TO-DATE
:processResources UP-TO-DATE
:classes UP-TO-DATE
:jar UP-TO-DATE
```

```
:publishPublishJarPublicationToArtifactoryRepository
```

Upload http://localhost:8081/artifactory/libs-release-local/book.gradle/
sample/2.1.DEVELOPMENT/sample-2.1.DEVELOPMENT.jar

Upload http://localhost:8081/artifactory/libs-release-local/book.gradle/
sample/2.1.DEVELOPMENT/sample-2.1.DEVELOPMENT.jar.sha1

Upload http://localhost:8081/artifactory/libs-release-local/book.gradle/
sample/2.1.DEVELOPMENT/ivy-2.1.DEVELOPMENT.xml

Upload http://localhost:8081/artifactory/libs-release-local/book.gradle/
sample/2.1.DEVELOPMENT/ivy-2.1.DEVELOPMENT.xml.sha1

```
BUILD SUCCESSFUL


Total time: 12.214 secs
```

When we open the Artifactory web application in a web browser, we can see that our project is now part of the repository, as shown in the following screenshot:

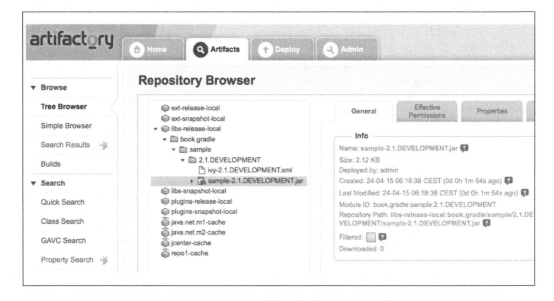

Publishing to Nexus

Another repository manager is Nexus. To publish to a Nexus repository manager is not much different from publishing to Artifactory or the local directory. We only have to change the `url` property to reference the repository and set the correct optional security credentials.

In the following example build file, we use a Nexus repository manager:

```
apply plugin: 'ivy-publish'
apply plugin: 'java'

version = '2.1.DEVELOPMENT'
group = 'book.gradle'

repositories {
  jcenter()
}

dependencies {
  compile 'org.springframework:spring-context:4.1.4.RELEASE'
}

publishing {

  publications {
    publishJar(IvyPublication) {
      module = 'sample'

      from components.java
    }
  }

  // Add a Nexus repository for
  // the publications.
  repositories {
    ivy {
      name = 'nexus'
      url = "http://localhost:8081/nexus/content/repositories/
releases"
```

```
        credentials {
          username = 'admin'
          password = 'admin123'
        }
      }
    }
  }
```

This time, the `publishPublishJarPublicationToNexusRepository` task is created. The task is also added as a task dependency to the `publish` task. The following code shows this:

```
$ gradle publishPublishJarPublicationToNexusRepository

:generateDescriptorFileForPublishJarPublication

:compileJava UP-TO-DATE

:processResources UP-TO-DATE

:classes UP-TO-DATE

:jar UP-TO-DATE

:publishPublishJarPublicationToNexusRepository

Upload http://localhost:8081/nexus/content/repositories/releases/book.
gradle/sample/2.1.DEVELOPMENT/sample-2.1.DEVELOPMENT.jar

Upload http://localhost:8081/nexus/content/repositories/releases/book.
gradle/sample/2.1.DEVELOPMENT/sample-2.1.DEVELOPMENT.jar.sha1

Upload http://localhost:8081/nexus/content/repositories/releases/book.
gradle/sample/2.1.DEVELOPMENT/ivy-2.1.DEVELOPMENT.xml

Upload http://localhost:8081/nexus/content/repositories/releases/book.
gradle/sample/2.1.DEVELOPMENT/ivy-2.1.DEVELOPMENT.xml.sha1


BUILD SUCCESSFUL


Total time: 5.746 secs
```

When we take a look at the Nexus web application inside the repository, we can see that our project is added to the repository, as shown in the following screenshot:

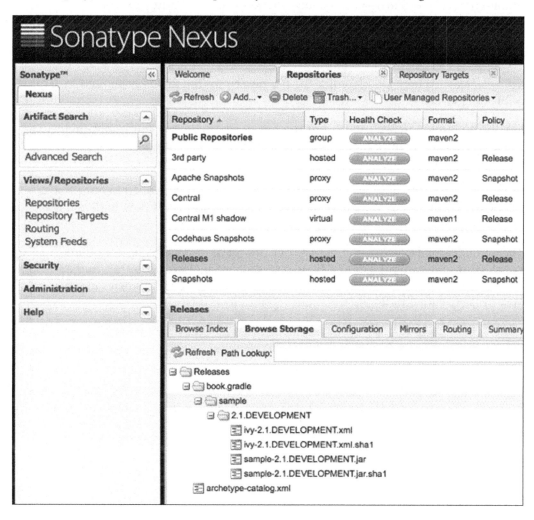

Summary

In this chapter, you learned how to use the new and incubating `ivy-publish` plugin. You saw how we can declare our publications with the `publications` configuration block. Gradle will automatically create new tasks based on what we have declared as publications.

You also learned how to customize the Ivy descriptor file that is generated by Gradle publishing tasks.

Finally, you saw how we can configure repositories to deploy our publications to. We used a local directory using the `file` protocol, and we used the Artifactory and Nexus repository managers.

In this book, we saw how we can define the dependencies we need in our project. You learned how to customize the dependency resolution and how to define the repositories that store the dependencies.

Then, you learned how we can deploy our project as dependencies for others. We saw how we can publish to a Maven repository, including Bintray, and an Ivy repository. You now have the knowledge to manage dependencies in your Java projects with Gradle.

Index

A

Ant task dependencies 19
archive task artifacts, Ivy Repository publication
  about 143-146
  file artifacts, using 147
  software components, using 147
archive task artifacts, Maven Repository publication 99-102
artifact-only dependencies
  excluding 51
Artifactory
  publishing, to Ivy Repository 158-160
  publishing, to Maven Repository 118, 119
artifacts
  archive task, using 79, 80
  configurations, defining 75-77
  creating 83-86
  defining 78
  files, using 80-82
  publishing, to local directory 87-91
  signing 92
  signing, archive tasks used 94, 95
  signing, configurations used 92-94
artifacts, types
  AbstractArchiveTask 78
  File 78
  Map 78

B

Bintray plugin
  about 125

configuring 135-138
defining 127, 128
new repository, defining 126, 127
publishing to 129-136
buildscript dependencies 17, 18

C

client module dependencies 9, 10

D

dependencies
  about 13-15
  accessing 16
  Ant task dependencies, optional 19
  buildscript dependencies 17, 18
  client module dependencies, defining 9
  client module dependencies 4
  configurations, declaring 1-4
  declaring 4
  dynamic versions, using 12, 13
  external module dependencies 4-9
  file dependencies, defining 11
  file dependencies 4
  Gradle API dependency 5
  Groovy dependencies, using 11, 12
  internal Gradle, using 11, 12
  local Groovy dependency 5
  managing 20-22
  project dependencies, using 10
  project dependencies 4
  types 4, 5
  version conflict, resolving 51

Thank you for buying
Gradle Dependency Management

About Packt Publishing

Packt, pronounced 'packed', published its first book, *Mastering phpMyAdmin for Effective MySQL Management*, in April 2004, and subsequently continued to specialize in publishing highly focused books on specific technologies and solutions.

Our books and publications share the experiences of your fellow IT professionals in adapting and customizing today's systems, applications, and frameworks. Our solution-based books give you the knowledge and power to customize the software and technologies you're using to get the job done. Packt books are more specific and less general than the IT books you have seen in the past. Our unique business model allows us to bring you more focused information, giving you more of what you need to know, and less of what you don't.

Packt is a modern yet unique publishing company that focuses on producing quality, cutting-edge books for communities of developers, administrators, and newbies alike. For more information, please visit our website at www.packtpub.com.

About Packt Open Source

In 2010, Packt launched two new brands, Packt Open Source and Packt Enterprise, in order to continue its focus on specialization. This book is part of the Packt Open Source brand, home to books published on software built around open source licenses, and offering information to anybody from advanced developers to budding web designers. The Open Source brand also runs Packt's Open Source Royalty Scheme, by which Packt gives a royalty to each open source project about whose software a book is sold.

Writing for Packt

We welcome all inquiries from people who are interested in authoring. Book proposals should be sent to author@packtpub.com. If your book idea is still at an early stage and you would like to discuss it first before writing a formal book proposal, then please contact us; one of our commissioning editors will get in touch with you.

We're not just looking for published authors; if you have strong technical skills but no writing experience, our experienced editors can help you develop a writing career, or simply get some additional reward for your expertise.

[PACKT] open source
community experience distilled
PUBLISHING

Gradle Effective Implementation Guide

ISBN: 978-1-84951-810-9   Paperback: 382 pages

Empower yourself to automate your build

1. Learn the best of Gradle.

2. Work easily with multi-projects.

3 Apply Gradle to your Java, Scala and Groovy projects.

Mastering Web Application Development with AngularJS

ISBN: 978-1-78216-182-0   Paperback: 372 pages

Build single-page web applications using the power of AngularJS

1. Make the most out of AngularJS by understanding the AngularJS philosophy and applying it to real-life development tasks.

2. Effectively structure, write, test, and finally deploy your application.

3. Add security and optimization features to your AngularJS applications.

4. Harness the full power of AngularJS by creating your own directives.

Please check **www.PacktPub.com** for information on our titles

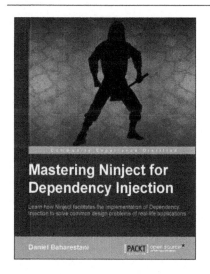

Made in the USA
Coppell, TX
27 February 2021